Given in memory of Dr. William (Bill) Horton, Professor of music, Organist, Shawnee, Oklahoma.

Basic Studies in Music

WILLIAM H. BAXTER, JR.

Professor of Music
Birmingham-Southern College

ALLYN AND BACON, Inc.
Boston

Preface

THIS BOOK ASSUMES little or no previous training in music theory. Much of it has been tested in a trial edition at Birmingham-Southern College for a period of six years.

I have made a special effort to define specialized terms clearly and precisely, but also in such a way that the definition is not limited to a single musical style or idiom. Lists of terms are included at the ends of the chapters. In those cases where conflicting terminology is in widespread use I have stated my preference, but in so doing I have attempted not to be dogmatic.

The symbols used for functional analysis in this book are those in common use in the United States. Figured bass, however, is discussed in the historical context of thorough-bass usage; thus, bass figuration is treated as a system of chord notation quite separate from chord function.

Four-voice writing is explained as part of a larger context in what might be called a textural approach to analysis and composition. In this way simple counterpoint is introduced as a natural part of elementary harmony. The textural concept makes it easier for students to relate their study of theory to the actual music they are performing. It also makes many fundamental concepts applicable to styles other than traditional harmonic writing.

Because I believe that an elementary theory course should give a broad base of musical information along with the usual concepts of part writing, I have included brief sections on the nature of serious music study, on simple acoustics, and on the principal units of musical form. In the early chapters the assignments are designed as drill for the memorization and use of necessary factual information. Exercises in later chapters offer more opportunity for creative work.

William H. Baxter, Jr.
Birmingham, Alabama

Table of Contents

v

1

The Study
of Music

THE STUDY OF MUSIC, like the study of any other art, is undertaken because of widely different motivations. For some, music is merely a pleasant recreation, leading at most to a lasting avocation; for others, it is a professional career involving a lifetime of work and dedication. Some students are impelled so strongly to study music that no other career is possible, while, for many, music is merely a means of doing what they like to do. Who should study music, and for whom should music be a professional career? The enjoyment of hearing music is a pleasure available to almost anyone who will take the time to learn to listen. Although not everyone realizes it, one must learn to listen, just as one learns other skills. Most students, with diligent practice, can learn to play a musical instrument or sing. A few, those with the greatest talent and dedication, can learn to play or sing well enough to make a career in one of the many fields of music.

How far a student can or wants to go in the study of music depends on his talent, diligence, personality, and many other factors, each of which can affect his performing and his possibilities of success. Musical talent or aptitude is an all-important characteristic of the good music student. Many people believe that some individuals have musical talent while others do not, but this is just not so; everyone *has* musical talent, just as everyone *has* height or weight. Most people have a reasonable amount of talent, while a very few have great talent, and a very few have almost no talent at all. The whole question is not whether one *has* or *does not have* talent, but just *how much* of this precious gift one has inherited. Many people make a living in music with ordinary talent, but almost none achieve greatness without exceptional musical aptitude.

A successful musician needs not only talent but temperament. Temperament, while necessarily related to musical talent, is also involved with the complex personality traits of the performer. Although temperament often seems intangible, it is a very real quality, essential to the performer and to the performance. It does not, in any case, mean mere eccentricity, or artiness, or the ability to lose one's temper. *Temperament is best defined as a person's ability to conceive how music should sound, and his unwillingness to have it sound otherwise.*

COLLEGE DEGREES IN MUSIC

One's purpose in studying music largely determines the degree for which he will work while in college. The student who desires a career as a professional performer, a college teacher of music, a church musician, or a private music teacher would normally work toward the Bachelor of Music degree, which emphasizes the ability to play or sing, and includes music courses necessary for an understanding of the whole realm of music. All music students will find it necessary and useful to study piano, whether this is their principal instrument or not. This is a professional degree enriched to some extent by courses in liberal arts subjects.

Some schools confer the Bachelor of Science degree to students who undertake a professional curriculum in music. Although schools differ in specific requirements, the Bachelor of Science degree in music is roughly comparable to the Bachelor of Music degree.

The student for whom music will be an avocation would normally consider the Bachelor of Arts degree. The major may be either music or some other discipline. There is little emphasis on individual performance skills in this degree; rather, the student learns to understand and enjoy music in the same way that he would study literature without attempting a professional course in writing. Strong in liberal arts subjects, the Bachelor of Arts degree is primarily for the student who does not expect to earn his living through music.

Students who desire the professional training of the Bachelor of Music degree, but who also want the broader educational base of the Bachelor of Arts degree, may, in some schools, undertake a five-year program leading to both degrees. Such a program provides both a general education and the specialized skills necessary for adequate professional music training.

The Bachelor of Music Education degree is a professional degree for students who specifically plan to teach in elementary or secondary schools. The college curriculum is usually based on state requirements for teacher certification. Although some specialization on one major instrument is normally required, the program in performance skills is less intense than that for the Bachelor of Music degree; moreover, performance skills are often spread among several instruments. Much time is spent in non-music courses in a number of different fields, with emphasis on educational methods.

A certificate in piano, voice, or other instrument is awarded in some professional schools to students who study only music; however more general courses are necessary in order to earn a baccalaureate degree.

Let us suppose for a moment that our music student has developed each of the many skills required of the musician. How does he make a living once he is through school? It is surprising that so many students aspire to careers as concert performers, but so few realize the monumental physical and mental skills required to achieve real competence. It is unfortunate that only a small fraction of competent recitalists can depend on concert performances to make their living. The professional musician, whether recitalist, orchestral player, or member of a dance band, often leads a precarious life of short-run jobs or one-night stands. His work involves constant travel, with consequent difficulties in maintaining a home and a normal family situation. After agents' fees and traveling costs are paid, the financial rewards are meager for all except a few public favorites. Unless he is one of these, the recitalist has a short career, after which he must find another source of income, often teaching.

Some music students prepare themselves for college music teaching by enrolling in graduate school. A career in teaching is less glamorous than one in performing, but there is greater long-term security. Salaries are moderate, but there are many fringe benefits. Such a career depends upon scholastic aptitude for success, for it requires at least a master's degree and often a doctorate. Preparation for college teaching should involve performance as well as the development of competence in the theory, history, and literature of music. However, a college has a right to expect its faculty to maintain an intellectual interest in the whole area of learning. A broad educational background is imperative in any college or university environment.

Teaching in elementary or high school requires a diversified musical education with less specialization on one instrument; the public school music teacher is often required to take charge of quite varied musical activities. Certification by a state board of education is necessary to teach in public schools and in many private schools. Public school music teaching is a highly specialized field, in which jobs are plentiful and usually permanent, once a teacher has made a start. Although salaries are frequently low, most school systems have retirement and insurance programs, and other benefits. The position of a teacher is an extremely influential one, calling for unselfish devotion and wisdom in dealing with others. Its primary reward comes from the satisfaction of influencing children and young people in the right way.

A musician who teaches privately, without the support of a school or other institution, may find it difficult to earn his living, although it is not such a severe problem for a teacher with an established reputation. Private teaching is, however, quite satisfactory on a part-time basis; it is, for instance, one of the few ways in which a woman can earn money in her own home. It can be easily combined with caring for a house and family, for the part-time teacher can spend as much or as little time in teaching as she wishes. Many such part-time teachers do a very efficient job within the limits of their training. The best preparation for private teaching is thorough training in performance and in music literature, along with a well-rounded general education.

Two fields, church music and dance music, have not yet been discussed. A full-time church musician must have thorough training either as an organist or as a singer; in either case he must be a competent choral director and be able to accompany on the piano or organ. The first qualification for any church musician is a deep, well-founded religious belief, but there is no place for the fanatic, or for the enthusiastic but uninformed believer. Musical competence is no less necessary because of strong religious dedication; *both* are necessary in this field. The church musician must be especially able to work with other people with enthusiasm and tact.

Directing or playing in a dance band or combo requires special skill in performing jazz, a skill most easily acquired through extensive experience. Dance band musicians are paid at least the union minimum scale, but bookings may be irregular; hours are long and mostly at night. Whether such a career is musically satisfying depends on the musician and the situation. Unfortunately, most dance band playing is routine repetition of popular hit songs; only rarely can a dance group rise to a level of artistic improvisation that excites widespread admiration.

PROBLEMS IN MUSIC STUDY

A number of problems peculiar to the study of music are often not fully recognized by the beginning student. Music is an art that exists in time, not in space. Unlike architecture or painting, or even literature, music will not stand still while we listen and re-listen. In a very real sense, music exists only in the memory of what has just been heard, and in the anticipation of what will be heard. The printed music score is merely an inexact blueprint of a sound that exists only at the time of the actual performance, then rapidly dies away. Moreover, unlike the painter or poet, the composer does not communicate directly with the listener. The composer merely draws the plan; that plan must then be relayed to the listener by a performer, much as a foreign language sometimes requires a translator. The painter paints on his canvas and presents it for the view of the onlooker. The poet or novelist writes, and his audience may then read. The composer writes his score, but it may take an orchestra of a hundred, under a trained conductor, to present the music to the listener. The relationship of the performer to the composer and to the listener creates innumerable problems, some of which have never been adequately solved.

One of the first barriers faced by the music student is the problem of physical learning. The physical skill necessary to play a musical instrument or to sing is similar to the skill needed for juggling or tumbling; it must be developed over an extremely long period of time, preferably during the physical growth period. Great concert violinists usually have started on the violin in pre-school years. With the possible exception of the virtuoso heyday in the nineteenth century, no previous period in history has required as much technical skill of pianists and violinists as the present. Such technical skill takes years to develop. Singers, particularly men, are at a distinct disadvantage in this respect because many of them do not become interested in singing until their teens. They must then work diligently to develop physical coordination and strength in the short period of growth and learning before adulthood.

Another instrinsic problem of music is its nonverbal nature. Although music is essentially a means of communication, it is not as specific or as rational as a language of words. Musical ideas can be imparted only crudely and imperfectly by spoken language. A teacher can use words to describe the structure of a musical phrase; he may, by words, convey to the student his conception of the meaning of the phrase; but only by playing it or singing it can he adequately express the content of the music.

LEARNING TO LISTEN

American civilization surrounds everyone with music; radio and television emit an endless flow of sound—even as background in dramatic programs. One is confronted with recorded music in restaurants, supermarkets, train stations, and even dentists' offices. The only defense against this continuous barrage of sound is to learn *not* to listen. Of course, background music is not designed to be listened to, but in shutting it out, one unconsciously learns to shut out serious music as well—music that requires not only hearing but listening as well. The musician must, therefore, try to form the habit of actively listening to music he once only passively heard. Active listening requires great concentration; it requires one to remember musical ideas as they are played. The form and shape of the piece is then reconstructed in the listener's memory. Knowledge of what to expect makes the listening process much easier: a knowing listener expects certain things to occur in a well established musical form; this guides his listening. Similarly, the ability to recognize each musical instrument by its sound is an asset in listening, for this gives a definite sound image with which melody, harmony, and rhythm may be associated. The intent of a good listener is to hear as much of the music as possible, including melody, harmony, rhythm, tone quality, musical texture, form, and of course the emotional and aesthetic content of the music. Such listening is an acquired skill, developed only over a period of years and by great diligence.

The necessity for concentrated listening applies not only to music performed by others, but also to music performed by oneself. The weak musician hears little, so there is little to correct. The good musician listens to himself with an intent ear and is thereby able to improve his own peformance.

LEARNING TO PRACTICE

Every teacher has students with fine talent, who never learn to play or sing well because they are not diligent or skillful enough in practice. Of course, talent is necessary, but just as practice without talent is a struggle with little hope, talent without practice is a waste of ability. Practice takes time—a great deal of time—because learning to play or sing is not just mental learning, but physical learning as well. Muscles have to be strengthened; coordination has to be developed. This can be done only by routine daily practice. Moreover, it is in the practice room that a student must learn to listen, to analyze, and to transform the printed plan of the composer into the structure of living music.

The experience of student after student has been that practice is one of the hardest musical skills to master. So often the practice period is taken up with playing rather than practicing the instrument. Practice is the time to repair what is wrong, to strengthen what is weak, to complete what is unfinished; it is a time in which the student teaches himself. How does one go about good practice? First, a student must form the habit of going to the practice room as one would go to a class. Practice must take precedence over extracurricular activities; it must not be put off until other things are done. It must be done daily, and for a sufficient period of time.

Many schools and conservatories establish minimum practice requirements for their students. Serious students will plan practice periods that far exceed minimum standards, but even long periods of practice will not accomplish what is desired if the practice is not the right type. Efficient practice utilizes the entire practice time for constructive purposes. Although repetition is necessary in practice, each replaying should have a specific goal. Moreover, repetition of short sections that cause difficulty is more useful than meaningless replaying of entire pieces. The efficiency of practice can be improved by setting specific goals for each practice period, followed by self-examination at the end of the period. It may take several periods to eliminate a problem, but clear goals and self-examination will make practice not only more gainful, but also more enjoyable.

A word should be said about mental practice, that is, thinking through a piece being studied. Although correct mental practice is difficult, it is the only way to develop conscious control in the mind, not merely in the muscles. In mental practice, every facet of performance must be imagined, including not only each note, but also dynamic levels, tempos, fingerings, and pedaling. Mental practice is extremely important, and it must be done in addition to regular physical practice.

AUXILIARY TOOLS IN MUSIC STUDY

The study of music begins with the composer's blueprint, the printed score, from which the performer conceives what the music is to be; but the musician who must play through a score in order to know the sound of the music is like an architect who has to build a house to know what it will look like. A musician must learn to read the score, that is, to conceive the intended sound merely by looking at the printed notation. This skill is of fundamental importance in the study of music. The music student needs to build a library of scores; by following these as he listens to music, he is better able to hear what goes on. This is the way many composers learned to compose; Wagner and Berlioz are notable examples.

Any serious music student must develop some facility in using the piano, regardless of his major field. Although few musicians not specializing in it would ever be called upon to give a serious solo performance at the piano, everyone in music needs to be able to use it as a tool in his work. Teachers specializing in orchestral instruments must be able to play accompaniments on the piano, at least in lessons. The singer constantly needs the piano in his own practice, as well as in teaching others. Anyone teaching harmony or other courses in music must be able to play musical examples. The piano is such a universal musical tool that laymen use the term "take music" to mean "study piano." The career musician without some piano ability is limited from the start, so the more facility at the keyboard, the better.

The advent of long-playing phonograph records, and more recently of stereophonic recordings, makes possible an acquaintance with music which only a quarter century ago would have required a lifetime of concertgoing to acquire. The great weakness of most beginning music students is that they have not heard enough great music. Every music student should have some kind of long-playing phonograph and his own collection of recordings, no matter how small. The collection should not be limited to his own field of performance but should reflect the entire literature of music. The amount of serious music available on television is far less than that available on radio, so the long-playing record and the live concert are now the principal means of becoming acquainted with musical literature. Of special help in this regard are the FM radio stations specializing in serious music, stations too often ignored by students and the general populace.

Another help to the music student is the metronome, a mechanical or electrical device for measuring even intervals of time. Any serious music student will sooner or later need to have one. Older models depend on a clockwork mechanism, while more recent types employ electric motors or electronic circuits. Clockwork metronomes occasionally need adjustment, and all metronomes need periodic care. Students should follow the advice of their teachers as to whether or not to buy metronomes.

OTHER THINGS TO KNOW

Some music students want to study nothing but their own instruments, or courses directly related to musical competence. Such an education is far too limited. Every student needs a broad educational background, in addition to specialized training in his own field. The first requisite of any educated person is the ability to read and write the English language with ease and clarity. This is a *basic* skill, as necessary for the musician as for anyone else. Like skill in musical performance, it can be obtained only by constant practice. Nor is English the only language required for the competent musician; all the European languages are helpful, not only because of musical terms borrowed from these languages, but because musicians frequently meet and play with musicians from foreign countries. Many valuable music dictionaries and treatises have not been translated into English. A singer needs even greater knowledge of language than does an instrumentalist. Opera, though historically an Italian form, quickly developed German and French styles. Singers are expected to understand these languages in addition to English, and to sing operas or songs in them as a matter of course.

A mature aesthetic appreciation of music requires an acquaintance with other arts—painting, sculpture, literature, and the dance. Musicians need experience in understanding and, preferably, taking part in these sister arts. Emotional and artistic maturity is aided by reading poetry, short stories, and novels, and by painting, or studying paintings. The understanding and expression of emotion seems to be the peculiar province of the arts. Depth of understanding, and the ability to reveal that understanding through music, literature, or the visual arts is the basic requisite of the true artist. An awareness of beauty in other fields makes the musician more sensitive to aesthetic value in his own domain.

The study of music is one of the most demanding disciplines in all learning. It requires memory, reason, muscular development, and emotional maturity. The devotion of so many people through the centuries to an art that brings so little material gain attests that it is worth the effort. No field of endeavor can bring purer pleasure to so many, but it does require dedicated study. A young person, entering into the serious study of music, must examine his own motives and desires; then he can make of music what he will.

2

Sound and Pitch

MUSIC IS COMPOSED of sound and silence. Although everyone is familiar with many different sounds, the word *sound* is hard to define with precision. Psychologists define sound in terms of our own hearing; physicists, on the other hand, define sound in terms of the disturbance in air to which our ears are sensitive.

Sound begins with motion. Some object, such as a drum head, a violin string, or a door bell, is set in motion. If the sound is to continue for even a very short period of time, the object must move rapidly back and forth in a special type of motion known as *vibration* or *oscillation*. If this could be seen in slow motion, the movement would resemble the back-and-forth motion of a clock pendulum or of a metronome. The motion that causes sound, however, is much faster, moving back and forth as many as five to ten thousand times in a single second. As the object moves to one side it presses against the tiny particles of air next to it, much as a policeman presses back the crowd at a parade. In this way, the molecules of air are squeezed closer together. When the object moves in the opposite direction, the squeezed molecules flow to fill the empty space, as if the policeman had moved the restraining rope forward a foot or two.

The continued movement of the object creates a succession of squeezes and releases, technically known as *compressions* and *rarefactions*. When compressed, air molecules push against air molecules nearby, in the same way that the moving object originally pushed them. As a result, each compression and rarefaction is transferred, relay fashion, from one group of air molecules to others near it. They, in turn, pass the compression or rarefaction on to other molecules in a kind of chain reaction. The movement of these changes of pressure through the air is called a *sound wave*.

A sound wave is sent out in all directions from a vibrating body such as a drumhead, a violin string, or a doorbell. It should be noted that what is transmitted is not the air itself but a series of rapid changes in air pressure. The air as a whole does not move; the molecules of air merely move back and forth, acting as bearers of the sound wave. Their action may be compared to that of a group of men fighting a fire in a bucket brigade. The men do not change their positions, but they effectively transmit water from the well to the fire.

Sound waves move in air at a speed of about 1,100 feet a second, or almost 700 miles an hour; their speed is affected slightly by temperature, humidity, and atmospheric pressure. A sound wave moves over four times faster in water than in air, and even faster in solid materials such as wood or metal. The speed of sound is much less than the speed of light, which travels through the universe at the phenomenal speed of 186,000 miles a second. This great difference between the speeds of light and sound creates serious problems in musical performance if the players are some distance from each other. This is particularly noticeable if bands at two sides of a stadium attempt to play together under the same conductor, or if choirs at opposite ends of a church try to sing at the same time. The slow movement of sound sometimes causes problems even when the speed of light is not involved. In some pipe organ installations, there is an appreciable lag between the time the organist presses the key and the time he hears the sound.

Musical sounds may come from a number of sources. Some of the more familiar sound sources are the stretched string of the violin or piano, the vibrating column of air in an organ pipe or flute, the stretched membrane on the drum, the solid bar of the xylophone or chimes, and the vibrating reed of the clarinet or harmonica. Each of these sound sources receives mechanical energy in the form of plucking, striking, or blowing and transforms it into sound energy, in the form of a sound wave.

When a sound wave reaches the ear, some of its energy causes the ear drum to vibrate. The vibration is then mechanically transmitted by three small bones in the middle ear to that portion of the inner ear called the *cochlea*. In the cochlea, the energy of the sound wave is converted, in some way not yet fully understood, into tiny electrical impulses which are sent through the nerve system to the brain. By means of these tiny electrical impulses, the brain interprets and analyzes sounds so that our memory and our intellect may recognize, classify, and use them.

NOISE AND MUSICAL SOUND

There are many kinds of sounds—knocks, rustles, rattles, roars, whispers, speech— to name just a few. Musical sounds are characterized by their regularity of vibration and a clearly identifiable pitch. Noise is irregular or disorderly vibration. The distinction is not an absolute one, however, for some musical instruments, such as the snare drum, the bass drum, and the maracas might more properly be called noise makers. Moreover, from a psychological point of view, even the loveliest musical sounds become noise if the listener does not want to hear them; consider the neighbor's phonograph that is played too late into the night. The distinction, then, between noise and musical sound is relative and depends upon the listener and the circumstance.

LOUDNESS AND INTENSITY OF SOUNDS

Everyone knows from experience that some sounds are louder than others. The concept of loudness is far more complicated than most people think. First of all, one must distinguish the *loudness* of a sound from its *intensity*. Loudness is a psychological property of hearing, but intensity is a physical property of the sound wave itself. The intensity of a sound refers to the amount of energy that the sound wave carries, while loudness is the strength of our sensation upon hearing the sound. Let us examine each of these terms briefly.

The intensity of a sound is primarily dependent upon how far the source of the sound moves as it vibrates to and fro, measured from the position of rest. This distance is called the *amplitude* of vibration. If the sound source moves only a very small distance in its vibration, that is, if it vibrates with a small amplitude, the intensity of the sound wave will be small, and our psychological hearing sensation will be that the sound is not very loud. If the amplitude of vibration is large, the intensity will be greater, and the sound will seem louder to our ear. Illustration 2.1 represents a violin string as it vibrates to produce a soft and a loud sound.

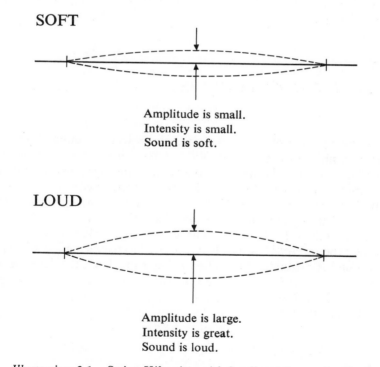

SOFT

Amplitude is small.
Intensity is small.
Sound is soft.

LOUD

Amplitude is large.
Intensity is great.
Sound is loud.

Illustration 2.1. String Vibrating with Small and Large Amplitude

The intensity of a sound wave also varies with the effectiveness of the sound source in transmitting its energy to the air particles near it. A small vibrating source will not move as many air particles as a larger one. A vibrating tuning fork will hardly be audible if it is held in the air, but it will emit a reasonably loud sound if placed so that it causes a larger object, such as a table top, to vibrate also. The greater intensity or enrichment of the sound results from a more rapid transfer of the original vibratory energy into sound waves in the air. The intricate construction of violins, pianos, and other musical instruments increases the efficiency with which the mechanical energy is changed into sound. *Resonance* is the quality of an instrument that can make this energy transfer efficiently. For the same amplitude of vibration in the string, a resonant piano produces a sound wave of greater intensity than one which is less resonant. A Stradivarius violin, being extremely resonant, may overbalance poorer violins because it tranfers the energy of the vibrating string into sound energy more effectively.

SCIENTIFIC UNITS OF INTENSITY

The intensity of a sound wave is measured scientifically in units called *decibels*, usually abbreviated *db*. The unit is of great importance in scientific studies of sound, in radio, television, and high-fidelity sound reproduction. The concept of intensity is of limited usefulness to the practicing musician, to whom loudness is far more important.

SCIENTIFIC UNITS OF LOUDNESS

Loudness is the strength of our sensation upon hearing a sound. Like intensity, it is a complex phenomenon that is affected not only by the intensity of the sound wave, but also by the pitch of the sound, the sensitivity of the ear, and several less important factors. Loudness levels are usually measured in units called *phons*. The human ear is amazingly sensitive—sensitive enough that it can hear sounds so soft that the amount of power that affects the ear is less than one millionth of one billionth of a watt. The softest sound that the human ear can detect is called the *threshold of audibility*; it is arbitrarily assigned a level of zero phons. If a sound is extremely loud, the ear begins to hurt; this level of loudness is called the *threshold of feeling* or the *threshold of pain*. With most people, pain occurs at a loudness of about 120 phons. The loudness levels of some common sounds are given in Table 2.1.

Table 2.1. Loudness Levels of Common Sounds

Threshold of audibility	0 phons
Quiet music	20 phons
Conversational speech	50 phons
Heavy traffic	70 phons
Full orchestra, fortissimo	90 phons
Boiler factory	100 phons
Threshold of pain (such as a jet plane exhaust)	120 phons

MUSICAL UNITS OF LOUDNESS

The loudness of musical sounds is an important aspect of performance. Not only are some pieces louder than others, but subtle differences in loudness make it possible to emphasize one melodic line more than another, to balance a chord so that its full harmonic value is felt, or to provide contrast between different sections of a piece. For the musical performer, the scientific loudness unit, the phon, is much too specific to be of practical value. At first, composers merely wrote into their manuscripts the words *loud* or *soft* in whatever language they were accustomed to use, but the Italian words *forte* and *piano* soon became common throughout Europe. As composers desired finer and finer gradations of loudness, they began to modify these basic adjectives, with the result that there is now a full scale of terms used to indicate loudness. In musical performance, these words convey relative rather than specific loudness levels. The *fortissimo* of stringed instruments is quite different from the *fortissimo* of the brass. Achieving a satisfactory balance or relative loudness is one of the tasks of any performer or conductor; it quickly reveals the artistry of the gifted. The scale of loudnesses now used in music may be seen in Table 2.2.

Table 2.2. Musical Loudness Levels

WORD	ABBREVIATION	MEANING
	ffff	Louder than *fff*
	fff	Louder than *ff*
Fortissimo	ff	Very loud
Forte	f	Loud
Mezzo forte	*mf*	Moderately loud
Mezzo piano	*mp*	Moderately soft
Piano	*p*	Soft
Pianissimo	*pp*	Very soft
	ppp	Softer than *pp*
	pppp	Softer than *ppp*

PITCH

When one listens to different musical sounds, some seem higher than others. The sensation of highness or lowness of musical sounds is called *pitch*. Pitch depends on the rapidity with which the sound source vibrates. Objects that vibrate rapidly produce sounds of high pitch, while those that vibrate slowly produce sounds of low pitch. In scientific fields, rapidity of vibration is measured by the number of vibratory cycles that occur in a single second. Each cycle is one complete vibration, which includes the motion both back and forth. The number of cycles in one second is called the *frequency* of vibration, measured by a unit called the *Hertz*, abbreviated as *Hz*. One Hertz is the vibratory rate of one cycle per second.

The human ear can hear sounds with frequencies as low as 16 to 20 Hz (cycles or vibrations a second), and as high as 16,000 to 20,000 Hz. Some animals can hear sounds of much higher frequency. Dogs are often called by a special whistle that is inaudible to the human ear. Bats and porpoises can hear sounds extending at times to 100,000 Hz. The sound of middle C on a piano has a frequency of 261.63 Hz, and the A by which an orchestra tunes is 440 Hz.

Even within the frequency limits of hearing, the ear is not entirely uniform in its reaction to sound. The ear is not as sensitive to very high and very low pitches as it is to sounds with medium frequencies of about 3,000 Hz. Modern high-fidelity phonographs have to compensate for this irregularity of the human ear by changing the balance between high and low sounds at different volume levels.

Although the designation of pitch by its frequency is highly accurate, the method is too cumbersome for musical use. The pitch of basic musical tones has for centuries been indicated by the letters A to G. The letter names are re-peated every eighth tone or *octave*, when the frequency of vibration has exactly doubled. Thus, if a tone with a frequency of 440 vibrations a second is called A, a tone vibrating 880 times a second, although higher, would simply be another form of A; frequencies of 220 and 110 Hz would similarly be called A, but would be in lower octaves. Notes exactly an octave apart, that is, notes whose frequencies are related by the ratio of two to one, sound very much alike to our ears. The musical notation of the western world has for centuries used the same letter name for notes an octave apart.

INFLECTION BY THE USE OF ACCIDENTALS

As music gradually became more complex, tones that lay between the letter names were indicated by signs called *accidentals*. The five accidentals that came into common use are listed in Table 2.3.

Table 2.3. *Accidentals in Musical Notation*

⋇	Double Sharp	Raises a tone two half steps
♯	Sharp	Raises a tone one half step
♮	Natural	Cancels other accidentals
♭	Flat	Lowers a tone one half step
♭♭	Double Flat	Lowers a tone two half steps

On keyboard instruments all of these variant forms are played on a set of black and white keys arranged in the pattern shown in Illustration 2.2. Natural notes are played with white keys; sharped and flatted notes, with black keys. Notes with double accidentals utilize the same key as the adjacent white note. Although C♯ is a half step above C, and D♭ is a half step below D, there was, in older systems of tuning instruments, a slight difference in pitch between these two notes. If the note was tuned to C♯, it was out of tune for D♭. The same was true in the similar situations that occurred between F♯ and G♭, between G♯ and A♭, and other such tones. Even today, string players and many other musicians play C♯ a little higher than D♭. Because it was impractical to try to maintain such minute differences in pitch on keyboard instruments, a system of tuning was

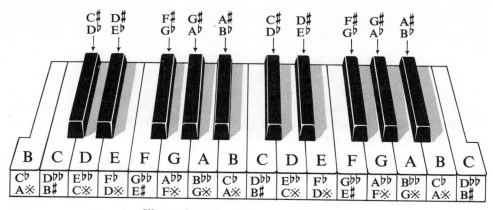

Illustration 2.2.   Notes on a Keyboard

devised that made it possible, by a slight compromise, to play such notes on the same key or string without retuning. This system, called *equal temperament,* divides the octave into twelve half steps, all the same size.[1] In equal temperament C♯ and D♭, G♯ and A♭, and other such tones have the same frequency even though they are named differently. Such notes are called *enharmonic tones.* Traditional harmonic usage does not consider enharmonic tones to be interchangeable, but treats each tone as a separate entity.

THE NOTATION OF PITCH ON A STAFF

The earliest methods of writing pitch were more suggestive than specific. Early music was learned by heart, but signs, called *neumes,* were placed above the words of the song in order to aid in memorizing the tune. Later the neumes were carefully heighted; that is, they were spaced higher or lower to give some idea of how high or how low each pitch was to be. As this notation by heighted neumes became more complex, one or more lines were drawn through the neumes to indicate certain fixed pitches. By the eleventh century the use of several such staff lines had been popularized by an important Italian musician named Guido of Arezzo. A four-line staff is still used in the notation of Gregorian chant. After experimentation with staves of four to seven lines, a five-line staff became standard by the sixteenth century, and this is the staff universally used today. The lines of the staff are counted upward; the first line of the staff is always at the bottom. Each line and each space in Figure 2.1 represents one note in an ascending order of pitches; accidentals are written to the left of the note, precisely on the same line or space that the note occupies.

---

[1] Half steps are the same size when the ratio of frequencies of the tones is the same, not when the arithmetic difference in frequency is the same. The ratio of the equal tempered half step is $\sqrt[12]{2}$, or approximately 1.059463. For example, to find the frequency of A♭, multiply the frequency of G by 1.059463. By an international agreement reached in 1939, the frequency of A above middle C on the piano was fixed at 440 cycles a second. In equal temperament, the frequencies of the pitches in that octave are: Middle C, 261.63; C♯ or D♭, 277.18; D, 293.66; D♯ or E♭, 311.13; E, 329.63; F, 349.23; F♯ or G♭, 369.99; G, 392.00; G♯ or A♭, 415.30; A, 440.00; A♯ or B♭, 466.16; B, 493.88; C, 523.25.

Figure 2.1

Music for the piano or for other keyboard instruments is written on a pair of five-line staves, each with its own range of pitches. The score of a piece for orchestra may require as many as fifteen or more such staves.

Ledger Lines

Whenever it is necessary to write pitches that lie outside the staff, short lines, called *ledger lines,* are drawn above or below the staff. Placed the same distance apart as the regular lines of the staff, ledger lines are drawn no longer than necessary to show a single note (Figure 2.2).

Figure 2.2

Use of Clefs

In order to use any staff, one of the lines must arbitrarily be assigned a certain pitch. This is done by writing a *clef* (from the French word meaning "key") on one of the lines of the staff. Other pitches are then located above and below, using both the lines and spaces created by the staff. A clef, then, is a sign that marks a particular line of the staff as a certain pitch. The clefs are modified forms of letters. The so-called *treble* clef, better named the *G clef*, and sometimes called *violin clef,* is really the letter G placed on the second (counting from the bottom) line of the five-line staff. Its presence shows that the second line is the G above middle C, as shown in Figure 2.3, and that other pitches are to be reckoned from that point of reference.

Clef sign was originally the letter G.      Clef shows that second line from the bottom is G above middle C.

Figure 2.3

The G clef is also used in a modified form like that in Figure 2.4 to indicate pitches an octave lower than the treble clef. The treble clef with a figure eight below it indicates that the second line is the G below middle C.

    G clef with 8 below it shows that second line is G below middle C.

Figure 2.4

Occasionally a double treble clef (like Figure 2.5) is used with the same meaning, although this is not generally accepted usage.

Two treble clef signs show that second line is G below middle C.

Figure 2.5

The *bass clef*, or *F clef*, is really an F placed on the fourth line of the staff; it signifies that the fourth line is the F below middle C, as shown in Figure 2.6.

Clef sign was originally the letter F.

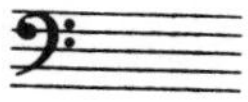

Clef shows that fourth line from the bottom is F below middle C.

Figure 2.6

Movability of Clefs

At one time each clef could be moved freely to any line of the staff, although this practice is rare in modern music. If the G clef were placed on the first line of the staff instead of the second, as in Figure 2.7, the bottom line would be G.

G clef in this position shows that bottom line is G. This clef is called the "French violin clef."

Figure 2.7

Similarly, the F clef could be moved to the third line, as in Figure 2.8, to indicate *baritone clef.*

F clef in this position shows that third line is F below middle C.

Figure 2.8

The Movable C Clef

The only clef that is moved in modern music is the C clef. Although rarely seen in piano music, the C clef is regularly used by orchestral players. The C clef indicates the position of middle C. In *alto clef*, shown in Figure 2.9, the sign is placed on the third line.

Alto Clef   Third line is middle C.

Figure 2.9

When the C clef is placed on the fourth line, as in Figure 2.10, it is called the *tenor clef.*

Tenor Clef Fourth line is middle C.

Figure 2.10

In older music the C clef was also found on the first line, called *soprano clef*, and on the second line, called *mezzo-soprano clef*. Figure 2.11 shows the beginning of the score for a Mozart string quartet (K. 387), with viola in its usual alto clef.

Figure 2.11.   Use of Alto Clef in String Quartet Score

In some music for male chorus published in the United States, the C clef is placed on the third space, like that in Figure 2.12. This irregular usage is not accepted by good music editors today, but is still sometimes seen. The clef is identical in meaning with the modified forms of treble clef; the sound is one octave lower than treble clef.

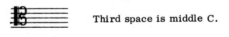 Third space is middle C.

Figure 2.12

Reading the C Clefs

It is important in reading the C clefs that one read not in relation to the bottom or top line of the staff, but *in relation to the position of the clef*. Thus, regardless of which line C happens to be on, the music is still read up and down from C. It is also important to remember that the C indicated by these clefs is not just any C, but is *always middle C*.

Because both tenor and alto clef appear to be one note more or less than an octave from treble clef, there is the temptation to read these clefs by transposing from treble clef. This should be resolutely avoided; *the notes in C clef are read by their relation to the C line, as marked by the clef*.

Since the letter notation for pitches is repeated in every octave, there must be some means of distinguishing the octave in which a certain A, D, or C happens to lie. The most commonly used system uses a capital C, called *great C*, to represent the lowest key on the organ keyboard, which is two octaves below middle C. The note one octave above is represented by a lower-case letter c, called *small c*. Pitches in successively higher octaves are indicated by lower-case letters with superscript numbers, such as c^1, c^2, c^3, etc. These pitches are sometimes written c', c'', c''', etc. Middle C on the piano is c^1. Doubled capital letters are used to represent pitches in the octave below great C, which is called the *contra* octave; CC indicates contra C. The next lower octave, the *sub-contra* octave, uses three capital letters. The full 88-note piano keyboard extends from AAA (sub-contra A), with a frequency of 27½ cycles a second, up to c^5, with a frequency of over 4,000 cycles a second. It should be noted that, through long custom, the change in octave name takes place not between G and A, but between B and C, as shown in Figure 2.13.

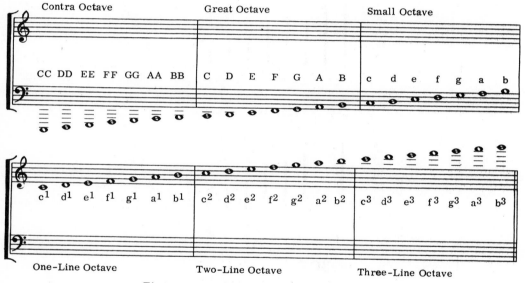

Figure 2.13. Octave Naming System

TONE QUALITY

Musical tones differ, not only in loudness and pitch, but also in *tone quality*. Although tones have so far been described as if they had a single, well-defined frequency or pitch, the sounds of music are rarely so simple. Every musical tone is not a single sound, but a complex group of sounds which the ear blends into one. Sources of musical sound vibrate not only at their *fundamental frequency*—the one we hear and identify—but also at frequencies that are twice, three times, four times the fundamental frequency, and so on. For instance, a musical sound with the fundamental pitch of A, or 440 cycles a second, also vibrates at 880, 1,320, 1,760 cycles, and other higher multiples of the fundamental. Each of the separate sounds in this complex is called a *harmonic partial*,[2] with the fundamental frequency being the first partial, and higher multiples of that fundamental being the second, third, fourth partial, and so on. The harmonic partials do not have equal intensities; their relative strength determines the tone quality, or *timbre*, of musical tones.

If a flute, clarinet, and oboe were to play the same fundamental pitch, they could each be identified by their individual timbres. This is possible because the strengths of the various harmonic partials are not the same for the different instruments. Illustration 2.3 is a graph of the strengths of the harmonic partials of these three instruments, all playing A, 440 cycles. The strongest upper partials on the flute are those that are one and two octaves above the fundamental. The clarinet, on the other hand, does not sound the second partial at all. Some of the higher partials on the oboe are stronger than the fundamental itself. Graphs such

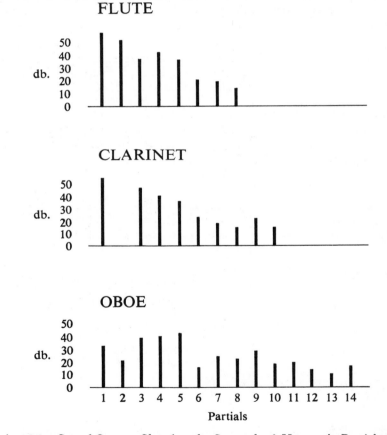

Illustration 2.3. Sound Spectra Showing the Strength of Harmonic Partials for Three Woodwind Instruments. (Each instrument is playing A–440. Partials not shown are so weak that they are negligible.)

---

[2] The term *overtone*, which means all partials except the fundamental, is not as satisfactory as *partial*. Since overtones and partials are numbered differently, the word *overtone* should be avoided.

as those in Illustration 2.3 are called *sound spectra;* they show the various components of sound in the same way that a prism divides light into different colors.

The relative strength of the different partials in the human voice determines not only the tone quality of the voice, but also the quality of the vowel that is said or sung. The vowel *ē* is strong in upper partials, much like the oboe, while the sound spectrum of the vowel *ōō* resembles that of the flute—it has weak upper partials and strong lower partials. Every speech sound, just like every musical instrument, has its own characteristic pattern of partials.

Some musical instruments are able to produce a number of different tone qualities; others produce only a few. The pipe organ has the greatest variety of tone qualities. Each rank of pipes has its own tone quality, which is immediately available to the performer. Most instruments produce a different tone quality in different pitch ranges. The low register of a clarinet, for instance, is rich and mellow, but its high notes are bright and piercing. The upper notes of a bassoon sound quite unlike the lower ones. Mutes, such as those used with trumpets or violins, affect the timbre of the instrument. Within the limits of a particular instrument, tone quality is primarily affected, however, by the performer's ability to recognize good tone quality and to achieve that quality in his own playing.

ESSENTIAL VOCABULARY

1. vibration
2. oscillation
3. compression
4. rarefaction
5. sound wave
6. cochlea
7. noise
8. loudness
9. intensity
10. amplitude
11. resonance
12. decibel
13. phon
14. threshold of audibility
15. threshold of feeling
16. forte
17. piano
18. fortissimo
19. pianissimo
20. mezzo piano
21. mezzo forte
22. pitch
23. cycle
24. frequency
25. Hertz

26. octave
27. accidental
28. sharp
29. flat
30. natural
31. double sharp
32. double flat
33. half step
34. whole step
35. quarter tones
36. equal temperament
37. enharmonic tones
38. neumes
39. staff (pl., staves)
40. ledger lines
41. treble clef
42. bass clef
43. alto clef
44. tenor clef
45. octave name
46. limits of hearing
47. fundamental frequency
48. harmonic partial
49. timbre (pronounced tăm-br)
50. tone quality

ASSIGNMENTS

1. A dead tree falls in the deep woods, but there is no one within a radius of ten miles. Does it make a sound? Discuss your answer.

2. Seated at one end of a stadium, a student sees the referee fire the starting gun for the quarter-mile relays. The student sees the puff of smoke from the gun, then about a second later he hears the shot. Explain.

3. Explain the difference between loudness and intensity of sound.

4. Write out definitions for words number 3, 4, 6, 8, 10, 11, and 12 in the vocabulary list above.

5. Define threshold of audibility and threshold of pain.

6. Define in your own words: pitch, frequency, octave, equal temperament, harmonic partial.

7. Using the frequencies given in this chapter, calculate the frequencies for each of the twelve tones in the octave whose lowest note is: a) the C two octaves below middle C; b) the C two octaves above middle C; and c) the second F below middle C.

8. The ancient sequence in Figure 2.14, *Victimae paschali laudes*,[3] is written in the notation used for Gregorian chant. If middle C is on the fourth line of the staff, what are the letter names of the notes in this excerpt?

Figure 2.14

9. Write the sign for each of the following clefs ten times each on a staff: a) G clef; b) F clef; c) alto clef; d) tenor clef.

10. Write the following pitches as whole notes on a staff (The whole note should be made in two strokes—⌒ plus ⌣ makes ○. See Appendix):

 a) In treble clef:
   a, a¹, e¹, f², c³, e♭¹, a♯², f♯¹, d♭₂, b♭.

 b) In bass clef:
   g, d¹, D, G, BB♭, B♯, f♯, c, e♭¹, a♭.

 c) In alto clef:
   f, a¹, c¹, e♭¹, b♭, g♯, e♯, g♭♭¹, d♯¹, f♭¹.

 d) In tenor clef:
   B♭, f♯¹, a¹, d, g♯, d♭¹, g, c, e♭.

11. Using treble clef, write the pitches two octaves above each of the following tones: F♯, g¹, a, BB♭, d.

12. Write whole notes in (1) treble clef and (2) bass clef to spell each of the following words:

---

[3] From *Plainsong for Schools* (Desclée et Cie., Tournai, Belgium), p. 83. Copyright 1933. Used by permission.

a) cab	f) fade
b) egg	g) beaded
c) fad	h) caged
d) bag	i) feed
e) faced	j) begged.

13. Give the proper letter and octave name for each note in Figure 2.15.

Figure 2.15

14. Write the pitches in Figure 2.16 one octave lower, using whole notes in bass clef. Give the letter and octave named for each new note.

Figure 2.16

15. Write whole notes in treble clef to give the same pitch as the notes in Figure 2.17. Give the letter and octave name for each new note.

Figure 2.17

16. Write whole notes in bass clef to give the same pitch as the notes in Figure 2.18. Give the letter and octave name for each new note.

Figure 2.18

3

Time and Its
Notation

FOR ORDINARY PURPOSES, time is measured by minutes, seconds, and hours. These units do not change; they are always the same. In music, the dance, and related arts, time is measured, not by a fixed or absolute unit such as a minute or a second, but by a variable unit called a *beat*. A beat is a pulsation that occurs at regular intervals of time. The beat is more felt than thought, more muscular than mental. It is easily recognized on the dance floor, in the marching of a parade, or in the rhythmic chant of a football yell. The beat is more vital than mere counting, which is a process of mentally calculating the relative lengths of notes. Counting is concerned with understanding the written notation; the beat is involved in performing the music notated. The count is mental; the beat is physical. There can be beats of different durations, so that the music may move slowly or rapidly. The rapidity with which beats occur is called the *tempo* of the music. The amount of variation in the length of a beat is not as large as is often supposed, but is limited to about the same speeds at which one can walk; one cannot really feel a single beat that is much longer or shorter than a walking pace. If one tries to walk very slowly, his step will be mentally subdivided into two or three faster beats, much as a bride divides her steps as she walks down the aisle. On the other hand, if a pulsation is very fast, one will automatically group two or three pulses into a slower unit that forms the actual beat. Rapid dancing normally involves grouping several steps into the regular physical beat of the music. In such cases the beat is the basic unit, but the individual dance steps subdivide the beat into several briefer intervals of time. Much music employs durations of time that are shorter than whole beats. Thus music employs time durations that are longer or shorter than a beat as well as durations that are equal to one beat of time.

THE NOTATION OF TIME IN MUSIC

The duration of tones is shown in musical notation by symbols of different shapes called *notes*. Different parts of the note include the *note head*, the *stem*, and the *flag* or flags. Silence is indicated by a corresponding set of *rests*. Notes and rests in use today are listed in Table 3.1.

Table 3.1. Names of Notes and Rests

NOTE AND CORRE-SPONDING REST			AMERICAN USAGE	ENGLISH USAGE	HISTORICAL TERM
ᴴ *or*	ᵟ	≡■≡	Breve or double whole note	Breve	Breve
𝅝		≡▬≡	Whole note	Semibreve	Semibreve
𝅗𝅥		≡▬≡	Half note	Minim	Minim
𝅘𝅥		𝄽 *or* 𝄾	Quarter note	Crochet	Semiminim
𝅘𝅥𝅮 *or* 𝅘𝅥𝅮		𝄿	Eighth note	Quaver	Fusa
𝅘𝅥𝅯 *or* 𝅘𝅥𝅯		𝅀	Sixteenth note	Semiquaver	Semifusa
𝅘𝅥𝅰 *or* 𝅘𝅥𝅰		𝅁	Thirty-second note	Demisemi-quaver	
𝅘𝅥𝅱 *or* 𝅘𝅥𝅱		𝅂	Sixty-fourth note	Hemidemi-semiquaver	

Each note and rest shown in Table 3.1 is twice as long as the note or rest below it. One whole note is equal in duration to two half notes; similarly, a quarter note has the same duration as two eighth notes, or four sixteenth notes, or one-half of a half note. Durations of silence indicated by rests correspond to durations of sound indicated by notes.

BEAT UNITS

In a particular piece of music, one note is chosen as the written symbol to indicate the duration of one beat. This is called the *beat unit*. Although the quarter note (𝅘𝅥) is commonly used, any type of note may serve as the beat unit. In older music the half note was the most frequent beat unit, while many modern composers use the eighth note. The symbol chosen for the beat unit theoretically does not affect the sound of the music at all, only its appearance on the page. Although the melodies in Figure 3.1 differ in appearance, they all represent exactly the same sounds; the only difference is the symbol used to represent one beat.

Although musicians by habit are likely to play the melody in eighth notes faster than the one in half notes, they should choose the tempo on a basis other than the mere notation.

Figure 3.1. Same Melody Using Different Beat Units

THE USE OF THE DOT

A *dot* placed after a note or rest indicates that the note is to be lengthened to one and a half times its original duration. Thus:

If ♩ equals 1 beat, then ♩. equals 1½ beats.

If ♩ equals 2 beats, then ♩. equals 3 beats.

If ♩ equals 1 beat, then ♩. equals 1½ beats.

If ○ equals 4 beats, then ○. equals 6 beats.

If ♩ equals ½ beat, then ♩. equals ¾ beat.

Sometimes two dots are placed after a note; this is called a *double dot*. The first dot adds one-half the value of the note; the second dot adds one-half the value of the first dot. The two dots lengthen the note to one and three-fourths of its original value. An undotted quarter note is equal to four sixteenth notes, but a double dotted quarter note equals seven sixteenth notes. Thus:

If ♩ equals two beats, and ♩. equals three beats, then ♩.. equals 3½ beats.

If ○ equals four beats, and ○. equals six beats, then ○.. equals 7 beats.

THE USE OF THE TIE

Times values cannot always be precisely indicated by the use of notes and dots alone. In some cases, two or more notes of the same pitch may be tied together by a curved line, like that in Figure 3.2, called a *tie*.[1]

---

[1] A tie is similar in appearance to the *slur*, which shows that two notes of different pitches are to be played *legato*, that is, smoothly and connected. A *phrase mark* looks like a long slur; it is used to indicate how notes should be grouped in performance.

The second note is not played or sung separately, but the first note is held through the value of both notes.

Figure 3.2

METER

In most of the music heard and played today, beats are grouped into patterns called the *meter* of the music; patterns of two, three, or four beats are spoken of as *duple*, *triple*, or *quadruple* meters. Occasionally one encounters patterns of five, seven, or even more beats, but these are not common. Moreover, some pieces of music move at such a pace that beats are heard individually rather than in groups. If only single beats rather than patterns are discernible, the meter may be described as *single*.

When music is written down, the meter is shown, sometimes precisely, sometimes less accurately, by vertical lines through the staff called *bar lines* or *measure lines*. The music between bar lines is one *measure* of music. See Figure 3.3.

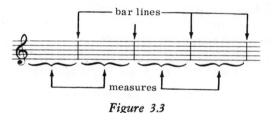

Figure 3.3

In Figure 3.4, the beats are grouped into patterns of two (duple), three (triple), or four (quadruple) beats, with each pattern separated by bar lines. Figure 3.4g has only one beat in each measure; this is an example of single meter.

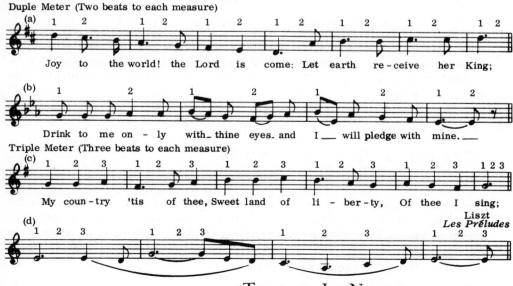

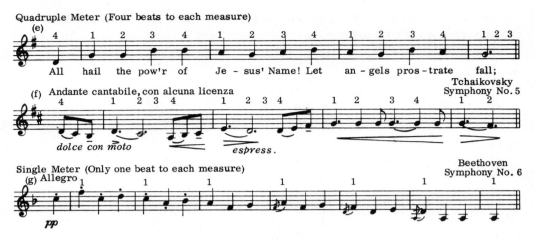

Figure 3.4. Patterns of Beats

SIMPLE AND COMPOUND BEATS

One other factor that affects the meter is the fundamental nature of the beats which make up the metrical groups. There are two basic types of beats—those that can be divided into two parts (or a multiple of two), and those that can be divided into three parts (or a multiple of three). The terms listed in Table 3.2 can be used to describe these basic types of beats.

Table 3.2. Terms for Types of Beats

DIVIDED INTO 2 PARTS	DIVIDED INTO 3 PARTS
Imperfect	Perfect
Binary	Ternary
Duple	Triple
Minor	Major
Simple	Compound

The terms *simple* and *compound* will be used in this book, since they are now the most frequently employed terms, and because there is less confusion with other musical terms in using these words. A *simple beat*, then, is a beat that can be divided into two equal parts. A *compound beat* is a beat that can be divided into three equal parts.

BEAT UNITS FOR COMPOUND BEATS

Since each written symbol for a note is either one-half or twice as long as the next longer or shorter symbol, it is difficult to use these symbols as units for compound beats, because a compound beat is divided into three equal parts rather than two. Dotted notes are therefore used for the beat unit when the beat is compound, because they are easily divided into three parts. Figure 3.5 shows the use of dotted notes as beat units.

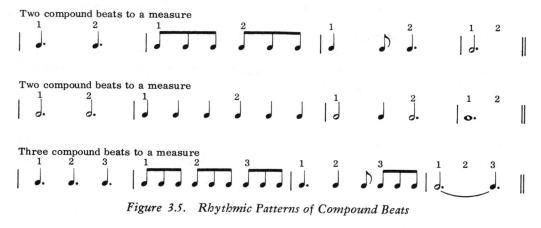

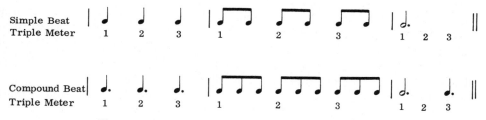

Figure 3.5. Rhythmic Patterns of Compound Beats

When triple meter consists of three compound beats, the pattern is quite different from that made up of three simple beats, as may be seen in Figure 3.6.

Figure 3.6. Patterns of Simple and Compound Beats

Because there is a difference between a pattern of simple beats and a similar pattern of the same number of compound beats, the terms *duple, triple, single,* etc., describe a meter only partially. To complete the description, one must also state whether the beats in the pattern are simple or compound beats. Thus to describe a meter fully, it is necessary to state 1) the nature of the beat (*i.e.,* simple or compound) and 2) the number of beats in each pattern of the meter (duple, quadruple, etc.) The most common meters are defined in Table 3.3.

Table 3.3. Commonly Used Meters

Simple single	One simple beat to a measure
Simple duple	Two simple beats to a measure
Simple triple	Three simple beats to a measure
Simple quadruple	Four simple beats to a measure
Simple sextuple	Six simple beats to a measure
Compound single	One compound beat to a measure
Compound duple	Two compound beats to a measure
Compound triple	Three compound beats to a measure
Compound quadruple	Four compound beats to a measure

TIME SIGNATURES

The meter of a piece of music and the notation to be used are usually indicated by a *time signature* placed at the beginning of the music. A time signature consists of two numbers, one above the other, such as $\frac{2}{4}$, $\frac{3}{4}$, $\frac{2}{2}$, or $\frac{9}{8}$. The time signature shows how many notes of a certain kind make up one measure. The signature $\frac{2}{4}$ indicates two quarter notes in a measure; $\frac{6}{8}$ indicates six eighth notes in a measure; $\frac{3}{2}$ indicates three half notes in a measure. The symbol C means $\frac{4}{4}$, and ₵ may mean either $\frac{2}{2}$ or $\frac{4}{4}$, depending upon the style of the music.

Unfortunately, the usual time signatures do not always indicate the kind of note that receives one beat, nor do they accurately indicate the number of beats in a measure. The number of beats—*real* physical pulsations—in a measure depends on the speed of the music as much as on the time signature. Although the time signature gives a hint, the meter must be deduced from 1) the top number of the meter signature and 2) the speed of the music. Performing musicians often speak of taking a particular piece "in four" or "in two," regardless of the time signature. A fast waltz with a $\frac{3}{4}$ time signature may be played "in one," meaning that the speed of the music is such that only one real beat is felt to each measure. To put this case another way, the performer thinks of the waltz, not in simple triple, but in compound single meter. With a time signature of $\frac{4}{4}$, there may be in actual use either two, four, or eight beats to the measure, depending on the speed of the music. Music in $\frac{6}{8}$ time is usually felt with two beats to the measure, not six. Moreover, it is not the eighth note but the dotted quarter that receives one beat. Similarly $\frac{9}{8}$ indicates three beats, and $\frac{12}{8}$, four beats to the measure. Bach, in one case, used a time signature of $\frac{24}{16}$ in a piece that is usually played with four beats to each measure. Handel's *Messiah*, on the other hand, requires eight beats to a measure in some pieces that are marked C. The meaning of commonly used time signatures at different speeds is shown in Table 3.4.

Table 3.4. Meters Indicated by Different Time Signatures

IF THE UPPER NUMBER IS:	ORDINARY SPEED	VERY SLOW SPEED	VERY FAST SPEED
2	Simple duple	Simple quadruple	Simple single
3	Simple triple	Three groups of simple duple	Compound single
4	Simple quadruple	Two groups of simple quadruple	Simple duple
6	Compound duple	Simple sextuple (two groups of simple triple)	Simple single
9	Compound triple	Three groups of simple triple	Compound single
12	Compound quadruple	Four groups of simple triple	Simple duple

The melodies in Figure 3.7 show different meters, some with simple, some with compound beats.

Figure 3.7. Melodies in Different Meters

Some pieces of music mix two different meters, although such mixing is unusual. In Figure 3.8, the singer has a melody with a compound beat, while the accompaniment has a simple beat; both parts have two beats to the measure.

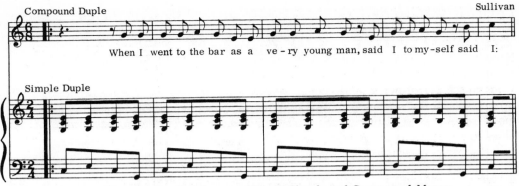

Figure 3.8. Simultaneous Use of Simple and Compound Meters

STRONG AND WEAK BEATS

When a metrical pattern has two or more beats, the beats are not of equal strength; some are more strongly accented than others. The first beat of each measure is the most intense; it is always the *downbeat* of the conductor's motion. In duple meter, the pattern is:

	STRONG	weak	STRONG	weak
DUPLE	1	2	1	2

Illustration 3.1

In triple meter, the third beat is the weakest:

	STRONG	weak	weaker	STRONG	weak	weaker
TRIPLE	1	2	3	1	2	3

Illustration 3.2

In quadruple meter, the pattern is:

	STRONGEST	weak	STRONG	weakest	STRONGEST	weak	STRONG	weakest
QUADRUPLE	1	2	3	4	1	2	3	4

Illustration 3.3

The amount of difference in the strength of the beats varies with the style of the music. At times the difference is barely perceptible; at other times it is very great.

PROPER GROUPING OF NOTES IN MUSICAL NOTATION

Because reading musical notation is not so much a process of reasoning as it is of recognition, it is essential that note values be written so that the meter is obvious to the performer at first glance. This is accomplished by putting notes into groups that form a whole number of beats. The problem of grouping appears most frequently in distinguishing $\frac{3}{4}$ from $\frac{6}{8}$, where the total number of eighth notes in a measure is the same in both rhythms. Note the difference between the two rhythmic patterns in Figure 3.9.

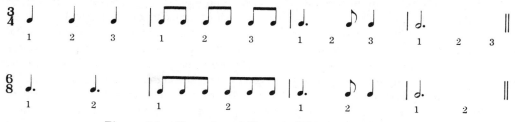

Figure 3.9. Grouping of Notes in Different Meters

In $\frac{3}{4}$, the eighth notes are grouped two by two, because two of them form a whole beat; in $\frac{6}{8}$, it takes three eighth notes to form one beat. Ties may also be used to clarify the intent of the music, even though the actual duration of the notes could be expressed by other means. The use of *beams* to connect eighth notes or other short note values is one means of indicating the proper grouping of notes. There are no hard and fast rules to determine the proper note grouping; it is more a matter of judgment. Compare the incorrect groupings in Figure 3.10 with their corrected forms.

WRONG   RIGHT

$\frac{4}{4}$ 𝅘𝅥𝅭 𝅘𝅥𝅭 𝅘𝅥𝅮𝅘𝅥𝅮
1 2 3 4

𝅘𝅥 𝅘𝅥𝅮𝅘𝅥𝅮𝅘𝅥𝅮 𝅘𝅥 𝅘𝅥𝅮𝅘𝅥𝅮
1 2   3 4

Figure 3.10. Correct and Incorrect Note Grouping

CONDUCTOR'S BEATS

The motions of an orchestral or choral conductor are reasonably well standardized, in patterns that indicate the number of beats in each metrical group of notes. Although the basic pattern of his arm movements may seem obscure to the untrained observer, the competent conductor communicates with the performers through patterns they recognize, no matter how many "flourishes" there may be.

Learning the conductor's basic patterns serves several functions. It is one of of the best ways to learn the metrical patterns and develop a feeling for them. Secondly, the ability to conduct these patterns helps greatly in reading new music. Lastly, the conductor's patterns are essential whenever one is called upon to take charge of any group of vocal or instrumental performers. Most musicians find themselves in this situation at one time or another, and they need to have at least a rudimentary skill in conducting.

The motion of the conductor's beat should be practiced until it is made easily, almost automatically. It is more than a mere pattern of movement; it is a pendulum-like swing, having a distinct feeling of muscular activity. Some people describe this by saying that each beat has a *point* or *pulse*, at which instant the beat begins; the end of each beat occurs with the beginning of the following beat. The standard conducting patterns are shown in Illustrations 3.4 to 3.7.[2]

1. ONE BEAT TO A MEASURE.   The pattern in Illustration 3.4 is used in fast tempos and in those styles of music that do not have a clear metrical pattern, such as some pre-classical music. The usual time signatures that use this pattern are: $\frac{3}{8}$, $\frac{3}{4}$, $\frac{3}{1}$, $\frac{3}{2}$, *or* $\frac{2}{4}$, $\frac{2}{2}$, $\frac{2}{8}$, all in fast tempo.

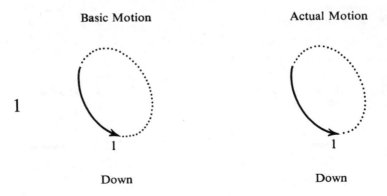

Basic Motion   Actual Motion

1

1   1

Down   Down

Illustration 3.4

---

[2] Left-handed persons usually conduct with the left hand, with motions that are mirror images of these right-handed patterns.

2. TWO BEATS TO A MEASURE. The pattern for duple meter, either simple or compound, is shown in Illustration 3.5. In moderate tempo, the time signatures would be $\frac{2}{2}$, $\frac{2}{4}$, $\frac{2}{8}$, $\frac{6}{8}$, $\frac{6}{4}$, $\frac{6}{16}$; in fast tempo, $\frac{4}{4}$ and $\frac{4}{8}$ would be included.

Basic Motion   Actual Motion

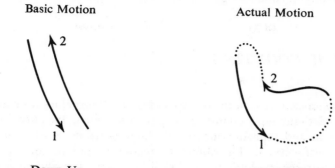

Down-Up   Down-Up

Illustration 3.5

3. THREE BEATS TO A MEASURE. The pattern in Illustration 3.6 is used in moderate tempo with the signatures $\frac{3}{4}$, $\frac{3}{2}$, $\frac{3}{8}$, $\frac{9}{8}$, $\frac{9}{4}$, $\frac{9}{16}$.

Basic Motion   Actual Motion

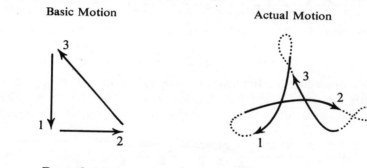

Down-Out-Up   Down-Out-Up

Illustration 3.6

4. FOUR BEATS TO A MEASURE. Illustration 3.7 shows the pattern to be used in moderate tempo with the time signatures $\frac{4}{4}$, $\frac{4}{2}$, $\frac{4}{8}$, $\frac{4}{16}$, $\frac{12}{8}$, $\frac{12}{4}$, $\frac{12}{16}$; in very slow tempos, the signatures $\frac{2}{4}$, $\frac{2}{2}$, and $\frac{2}{8}$ would be included.

Basic Motion   Actual Motion

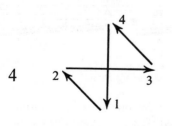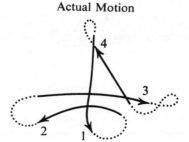

Down-Across-Out-Up   Down-Across-Out-Up

Illustration 3.7

TIME AND ITS NOTATION

There are a number of more complicated conducting patterns; measures with five, six, or seven beats, although not often used, are conducted by variations of the standard patterns. A full discussion of the more complex patterns must be left to books on conducting.

MUSICAL COUNTING

Musical *counting* is a means of expressing the time values in music by a combination of motions, taps, counts, and spoken syllables. Its purpose is to aid in the recognition and reproduction of rhythmic patterns as they are encountered in musical performance. The ability to recognize and perform a large vocabulary of such patterns is a basic musical skill, necessary for singing or playing at sight, and extremely helpful in memorizing music.

Most music students have been taught some rudimentary system of counting in their elementary music study. Some count by saying "one-and, two-and, three-and," as shown in Figure 3.11.

Figure 3.11

Since this procedure cannot express note values of less than half a beat, it is inadequate for any except the simplest music. The use of numbers to count regular subdivisions of the beat is somewhat more satisfactory, as in Figure 3.12.

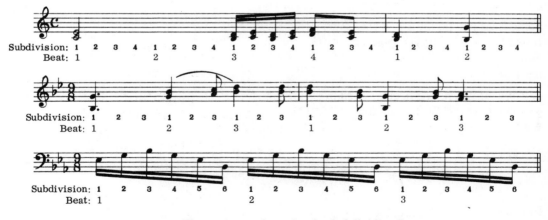

Figure 3.12. Counting by Subdividing Beats

This procedure is adequate for note values less than one beat in duration, but it still needs a sense of meter. When combined with a conductor's beat that indicates the metrical pattern, it forms an easily understood counting system. If notes are too rapid to be counted individually in this manner, it is possible to group several notes into one of the subdividing counts. In the "G major Prelude" from the first volume of the *Well-Tempered Clavier* by Bach, the right-hand part is so fast that it would be awkward to count each of the notes separately. By grouping three of the sixteenth notes together in each subdivision, this passage may be counted as shown in Figure 3.13.

Figure 3.13

TRIPLETS AND DUPLETS

Sometimes compound beats are found in music in which the basic pulse is simple. Instead of changing the time signature, it is more convenient and customary to indicate an irregular beat by a *triplet*. In Figure 3.14, the three eighth notes marked with a 3 occur within a single beat.

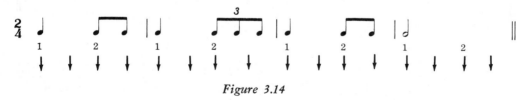

Figure 3.14

In Figure 3.15, the three quarter notes occur within a single beat.

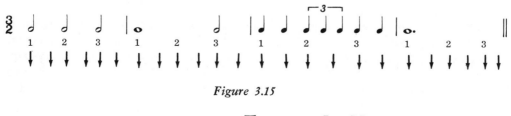

Figure 3.15

TIME AND ITS NOTATION   37

Occasionally one encounters a triplet that is spread over two beats instead of one, such as that shown in Figure 3.16. This is an ancient musical device, known for a long while by the term *sesquialtera,* a word describing three notes that occur in the time normally allotted to two. When this device occurs, the tempo must be slow enough for the triplet to cover two beats instead of one.

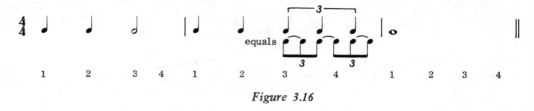

Figure 3.16

The use of a *duplet* in notation indicates that one or more simple beats occur in music that is predominantly compound in feeling. A duplet is the opposite of a triplet. See Figure 3.17.

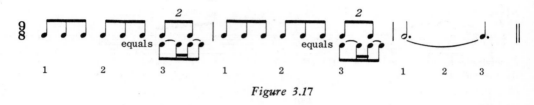

Figure 3.17

HEMIOLA

A shift in the grouping of notes from groups of threes to groups of twos with equal measure lengths is called a *hemiola.* This amounts to a shift from compound duple to simple triple meter. The device and the name for it are quite old, but it is still common today—in the rhumba, for instance, the hemiola may be counted within the basic meter, as in Figure 3.18.

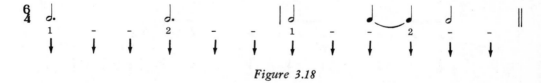

Figure 3.18

It may also be treated as a change in both tempo and meter, as indicated in Figure 3.19; the background pulse, here written as a quarter note, is of unchanging value.

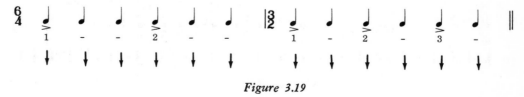

Figure 3.19

The hemiola was common in the time of Bach and Handel, and it is an identifying characteristic of the music of Brahms.

PICKUP NOTES

In many cases, a piece of music begins with only the last part of a measure. Any note (or notes) that precedes the first strong accent is called a *pickup* note, or more technically an *anacrusis*. It is customary in short pieces to deduct the value of such a note from the last measure of the music. When counting measures, an anacrusis at the beginning is disregarded; the first complete measure is counted as number one.

SYNCOPATION

Syncopation occurs when a note starts on a relatively unaccented beat or part of a beat and continues through a stronger beat. Syncopation is a frequent phenomenon in all kinds of jazz, and it is common in much serious music as well. In Figure 3.20, the notes marked with an arrow are syncopated.

Figure 3.20. The Use of Syncopation

The rhythmical structure of music has undergone many changes since 1900. Dissatisfied with traditional metric patterns, modern composers have experimented with a number of new rhythmic ideas that often require *unconventional note groupings*. In most of the new rhythmic patterns, the duration of some small note value, often the eighth note, remains constant, while the grouping of these short notes differs from that in conventional meters; the metrical pattern may vary in length from measure to measure. The excerpt in Figure 3.21 has a conventional time signature but an unconventional grouping. Note that one group even crosses the bar line.

Figure 3.21.   Unconventional Note Groupings[3]

The shifting metrical pattern in Figure 3.22 is reflected in the frequent changes of time signature. With the eighth note constant, the placement of bar lines is determined by the position of accented notes.

Figure 3.22.   Rapidly Changing Time Signatures[4]

Occasionally composers will use a double time signature, so that the meter may readily shift from one to the other. In Figure 3.23 the signatures $\frac{3}{4}$ and $\frac{6}{8}$ are used together, with the eighth note being of constant value. This is a modern notation for music that frequently employs hemiola, briefly discussed on page 38.

Figure 3.23. *Double Time Signature*[5]

Another innovation in rhythm is the *asymmetrical division* of the measure. Conventional meters divide a measure into equal sections, but asymmetrical division results in unequal sections. The dotted bar lines in Figure 3.24 indicate the grouping of notes within each measure. The time signature is written $\frac{8}{8}$, not $\frac{4}{4}$, since the latter customarily implies four equal groups of two eighth notes.

Figure 3.24. *Asymmetrical Division of Measure*[6]

Asymmetrical note groupings that regularly recur may also be indicated by a time signature such as that in Figure 3.25.

TIME AND ITS NOTATION   *41*

Figure 3.25.   Asymmetrical Signature[7]

One extremely useful modification of rhythmic notation is a new kind of time signature that specifies the beat unit more accurately than conventional signatures. First devised by Émile Jaques-Dalcroze, the new signature has been used by several modern composers, including Carl Orff. The upper number of the traditional signature is retained, but the lower number is replaced by the note symbol that represents one beat, as seen in Figure 3.26. A dotted note indicates a compound beat. The usual $\frac{3}{4}$ signature of simple triple meter becomes $\frac{3}{\flat}$; but

if the tempo is fast enough so that there is only one beat to a measure, the new signature would be written $\frac{1}{\flat\cdot}$, indicating simple single meter with one dotted

half note to the beat, and only one compound beat to the measure. Instead of $\frac{6}{8}$, the symbol $\frac{2}{\flat\cdot}$ is used to show that there are two beats to the measure and

that each dotted quarter note receives one beat.

Figure 3.26.   New Style Time Signature[8]

---

[7] *Mikrokosmos* (Volume VI) by Béla Bartók. Copyright 1941 by Hawkes & Son (London) Ltd. Reprinted by permission of Boosey and Hawkes, Inc.

[8] *Catulli carmina* by Carl Orff, p. 33. Copyright 1943 by B. Schott's Söhne, Mainz. Used by permission.

TEMPO MARKINGS

The composer indicates how fast his piece should be played by writing a descriptive term at the beginning of each section of music. For a long time it has been customary to use Italian words such as *andante, allegro,* and *adagio* for this purpose. Although these tempo markings are not in themselves better than English or German or French words such as *fast, slow, vite, langsam,* etc., the Italian terms have been used so long that musicians of all nations recognize and understand them. Dictionaries of musical terms define all these words, but a deeper understanding of a word is gained by finding out what that word meant in its original language before it became a musical term.

THE METRONOME

The metronome, invented by Johann Mälzel in 1816, is a clock-like mechanical device for measuring the duration of musical beats. In recent years, electrical metronomes have been devised. The metronome ticks loudly at a speed which can be adjusted as desired; a scale shows the number of ticks the device can make in one minute. Composers since the time of Beethoven, who died in 1827, have been able to indicate the tempo of their music very precisely by writing a metronome marking such as M.M. $\downarrow = 84$, or M.M. $\downarrow = 72$ at the beginning of the music (M.M. stands for *Mälzel metronome*). In the first example, there are 84 quarter notes to the minute; in the second, 72 half notes to the minute. The exactness with which a composer's metronome markings should be followed is a matter of dispute among performing musicians. Some feel that the composer's marking is only a general indication of tempo; others feel it should be followed precisely. Tempo markings are sometimes given as an approximate figure (M.M. $\downarrow = 76$–84), to allow the performer to choose the tempo for a particular occasion.

SETTING TEMPOS WITH A WATCH

An ordinary wrist watch or pocket watch may be used as a means of setting tempo. A watch makes five ticks a second; by choosing a certain number of ticks to equal one beat, a tempo can be set rather easily in accordance with Table 3.5.

Table 3.5. Watch Ticks and Metronome Markings

NUMBER OF TICKS TO THE BEAT	NUMBER OF BEATS TO THE MINUTE (EQUIVALENT METRONOME MARKING)
5	60
4	75
3	100
2	150

1. beat
2. tempo
3. breve
4. whole note
5. note head
6. note stem
7. half note
8. quarter note
9. flag
10. eighth note
11. sixteenth note
12. thirty-second note
13. sixty-fourth note
14. beat unit
15. dot
16. double dot
17. tie
18. slur
19. phrase mark
20. meter
21. duple meter
22. triple meter
23. quadruple meter
24. single meter
25. bar line
26. measure
27. simple beat
28. compound beat
29. time signature
30. downbeat
31. note grouping
32. beam
33. conductor's beat
34. counting
35. triplet
36. two-beat triplet
37. sesquialtera
38. duplet
39. hemiola
40. pickup note
41. anacrusis
42. syncopation
43. asymmetrical grouping
44. Dalcroze time signature
45. tempo marking
46. metronome
47. metronome marking

ASSIGNMENTS

1. Define a *beat*. How does it differ from a *count?*

2. Explain what happens if one tries to beat a pulse that is too fast or too slow.

3. Explain the difference between simple and compound beats.

4. The melodies in Figure 3.27 have an eighth note for each beat. Write the melodies again with a half note for each beat, then again with a quarter note for each beat.

Figure 3.27

5. Copy the examples in Figure 3.28. Add enough notes so that each measure will have the proper number of beats. Compensate in the last measure for the pickup note. Use care in grouping notes.

Figure 3.28

6. Copy the examples in Figure 3.29. Add or subtract enough notes so that each measure will have the proper number of beats. Dots may also be added to notes, or deleted. Use care in grouping notes.

a)

b)

c)

d)

e)

Figure 3.29

7. Rewrite the examples in Figure 3.30 so that each note grouping will be correct for its meter; keep the durations of tones precisely the same as shown. Each exercise represents one measure.

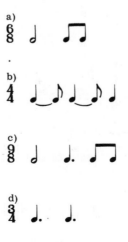

Figure 3.30

8. The excerpt from Palestrina's *Tenebrae factae sunt* in Figure 3.31 uses a whole note beat unit in the section marked $\frac{3}{1}$, and a half note beat unit in the section marked ¢. Rewrite it with a quarter note beat unit throughout, changing the time signatures as needed. Place note stems in the proper position to indicate soprano, alto, tenor, and bass voices.

Figure 3.31[9]

9. Give three traditional time signatures and one Dalcroze signature for each of the following meters. Indicate a suitable tempo marking for each of the four signatures.

[9] Copyright 1933 by Oliver Ditson Company. Used by permission of Theodore Presser Company, owners.

a) simple duple   e) compound duple

b) simple triple   f) compound triple

c) simple quadruple   g) compound quadruple

d) compound single

10. With the help of Italian, French, and German dictionaries, but without using a music dictionary, write out the basic meanings of the following words used to indicate tempo:

a) *allegro*   k) *langsam*

b) *andante*   l) *prestissimo*

c) *tempo giusto*   m) *meno mosso*

d) *schnell*   n) *vif*

e) *lento*   o) *larghetto*

f) *con moto*   p) *ritardando*

g) *accelerando*   q) *presto*

h) *vivace*   r) *moderato*

i) *largo*   s) *lent*

j) *più mosso*

4

Musical

Intervals

An INTERVAL IS the aural relationship between two musical tones. If the two tones are sounded at the same time, the interval is a *harmonic interval;* if one tone is sounded after the other, the interval is a *melodic interval.* An interval is identified by its *name* and by its *quality*.

INTERVAL NAMES

The more common intervals have the following names: *unison* or *prime* (terms used instead of *first*), *second, third, fourth, fifth, sixth, seventh,* and *octave* (a term used instead of *eighth*). These are shown in Figure 4.1.

Figure 4.1.   Common Intervals

The name of an interval is determined by counting the letter names from one note to the other, *always* counting the first note as number one. For example, to determine a sixth above F, the letter names are counted upward, like the arrow in Figure 4.2, beginning with F as number one. A sixth above F is D.

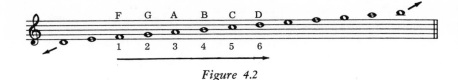

Figure 4.2

Similarly, to determine a fifth below B, the letter names are counted, downward this time, as in Figure 4.3, beginning with B as number one. A fifth below B is E.

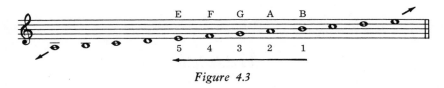

Figure 4.3

QUALITIES OF INTERVALS

A variation in the size of an interval, because of the presence of accidentals, determines the interval's *quality*. The accidentals that affect the quality of an interval do not change the letter names of the notes, or consequently the name of the interval. Regardless of accidentals, the interval from F to D, to take one example, remains a sixth. Thus, F to D♯, F to D♭, F to D✕, and F to D♭♭ are all sixths; only the qualities are different.

Some intervals have four possible qualities; others have only three. The intervals of the third, sixth, second, and seventh have four qualities, which are *augmented, major, minor,* and *diminished.* These qualities differ in size by one half step, as may be seen in Figure 4.4. Augmented is one half step larger than major; major is one half step larger than minor; minor is one half step larger than diminished.

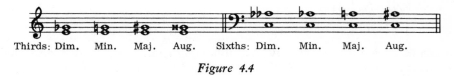

Thirds: Dim.　Min.　Maj.　Aug.　Sixths: Dim.　Min.　Maj.　Aug.

Figure 4.4

The intervals of the unison, octave, fifth, and fourth have only three qualities. which are *augmented, perfect,* and *diminished.* With these intervals, augmented is one half step larger than perfect, and perfect is one half step larger than diminished, as in Figure 4.5.

Fifths: Dim.　Perf.　Aug.　Fourths: Dim.　Perf.　Aug.

Figure 4.5

Intervals that have only three qualities cannot be major or minor, nor can the intervals that have four qualities be perfect. There is no major fifth or minor fourth, just as there is never a perfect third or a perfect seventh. The qualities of intervals are listed in Table 4.1.

Table 4.1. List of Interval Qualities

FOUR-QUALITY INTERVALS (third, sixth, second, seventh)	THREE-QUALITY INTERVALS (unison, octave, fifth, fourth)
Augmented	
Major	Augmented
Minor	Perfect
Diminished	Diminished

The qualities of intervals are defined in relative terms. Major, for instance, is defined as larger than minor and smaller than augmented. If one quality of an interval is known, the other qualities can easily be determined. The third from C natural to E natural is a major third; the thirds from C sharp to E or from C to E flat would then be minor, because each of these intervals is one half step smaller than the interval from C to E.

RULES FOR FINDING INTERVAL QUALITIES

The following rules for determining specific interval qualities should be memorized. The application of these rules is shown in Figures 4.6 to 4.12.

Unisons and Octaves

If both tones of the interval have the same accidental, unisons and octaves are perfect.

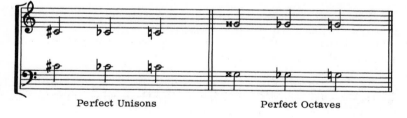

Perfect Unisons   Perfect Octaves

Figure 4.6

Fifths

If both tones of the interval have the same accidental, all fifths are perfect except the one above B, which is diminished.

Perfect Fifths   Diminished Fifths

Figure 4.7

Fourths

If both tones of the interval have the same accidental, all fourths are perfect except the one above F, which is augmented.

Perfect Fourths   Augmented Fourths

Figure 4.8

Thirds

If both tones of the interval have the same accidental, the thirds above C, F, and G are major; the others are minor.

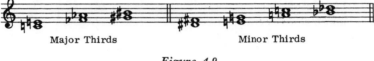

Major Thirds   Minor Thirds

Figure 4.9

Sixths

If both tones of the interval have the same accidental, the sixths above C, D, F, and G are major; the others are minor.

Major Sixths   Minor Sixths

Figure 4.10

Seconds

The second that consists of two half steps is major. The second that consists of one half step is minor. (*The two tones must not have the same letter name.* From C to D flat is a minor second, but from C to C sharp is an augmented unison.)

Minor Seconds   Major Seconds

Figure 4.11

Sevenths

The seventh that is one half step smaller than a perfect octave is major. (The major seventh is a very harsh-sounding interval, and one must not confuse it with the sweeter-sounding minor seventh.) The seventh that is one whole step or two half steps smaller than a perfect octave is minor.

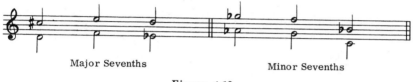

Major Sevenths   Minor Sevenths

Figure 4.12

ADDITION OF INTERVALS

Two musical intervals are added together when they are arranged so that the top note of one is the same as the bottom note of the other, like the intervals in Figure 4.13. The new interval that is formed between the lowest and highest tones of the combination is the sum of the separate intervals.

(F to C) + (C to D) = (F to D)

Figure 4.13

Unfortunately, the name of the new interval is not obtained by merely adding the names of the original intervals. Because one tone is common to both intervals, it is always necessary to *subtract one* from the sum of the names. In the example given above, the interval from F to C is a fifth, that from C to D is a second, and the interval obtained by adding them together is a sixth. Figure 4.14 should make the procedure clear.

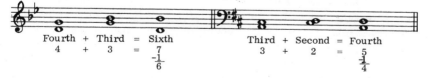

Fourth + Third = Sixth   Third + Second = Fourth

$$4 + 3 = \frac{\frac{7}{-1}}{6} \qquad 3 + 2 = \frac{\frac{5}{-1}}{4}$$

Figure 4.14. Addition of Intervals

INVERSION OF INTERVALS

If the tones of an interval are moved so that their positions are reversed, the upper tone becomes the lower and the interval is said to be *inverted*. The inversion of simple intervals, shown in Figure 4.15, is accomplished by moving the upper tone down one octave or by moving the lower tone up one octave. This is governed by a few simple rules:

1. The arithmetic sum of the names of the interval and of its inversion is always nine.

2. The inversion of a perfect interval is also perfect.

3. The inversion of a major interval is minor, and vice versa.

4. The inversion of an augmented interval is diminished, and vice versa.

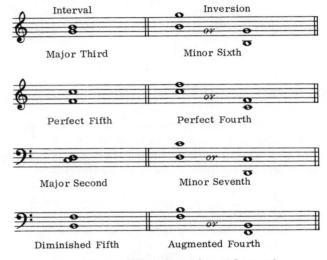

Figure 4.15. Simple Inversion of Intervals

COMPOUND INTERVALS

We have, so far, discussed only intervals smaller than an octave, called *simple intervals*. Intervals larger than an octave are called *compound intervals*. These larger intervals may be named by counting letter names just as with simple intervals. Thus we have intervals of the *ninth, tenth, twelfth,* and so on. Quite commonly, however, the octave in these intervals is disregarded, so that a tenth is called a third, or a twelfth, a fifth. The quality of the compound interval is the same as that of the simple interval to which it is reduced if the octave is disregarded. A major tenth is thus an octave and a major third; a perfect twelfth is an octave and a perfect fifth. The commonly used compound intervals are shown in Figure 4.16.

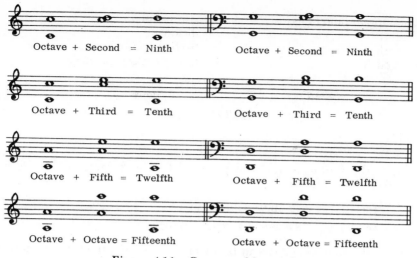

Figure 4.16. Compound Intervals

CONSONANT AND DISSONANT INTERVALS

In traditional music theory, *dissonant* intervals are those that give an impression of activity, so that they must be followed by other intervals. A *consonant* interval gives an impression of rest or finality. Dissonant intervals thus need to *resolve* to consonant intervals. A consonant interval is a *perfect consonance* if it retains the same quality when inverted. For instance, the inversion of a perfect unison is a perfect octave. Because the quality of both intervals is the same, the interval is a perfect consonance. An *imperfect consonance* changes quality when inverted; for instance, a major third inverts to a minor sixth.

There are three perfect consonances—the perfect unison, perfect fifth, and perfect octave. The four imperfect consonances are the major and minor third and the major and minor sixth. The dissonances include all fourths, seconds, and sevenths, and all diminished and augmented intervals.

ESSENTIAL VOCABULARY

1. interval
2. harmonic interval
3. melodic interval
4. interval name
5. interval quality
6. unison
7. prime
8. second
9. third
10. fourth
11. fifth

12. sixth
13. seventh
14. octave
15. augmented
16. major
17. minor
18. diminished
19. perfect
20. addition of intervals
21. inversion of intervals
22. simple intervals

23. compound intervals
24. ninth
25. tenth
26. twelfth

27. consonant
28. dissonant
29. perfect consonance
30. imperfect consonance

ASSIGNMENTS

1. Write the following tones in treble clef. Above each tone write another tone a perfect fourth higher.

    1) f♯² 2) a♯ 3) d♭¹ 4) b♭ 5) c¹
    6) e² 7) g♯¹ 8) a♭¹ 9) b♯¹ 10) d♯²

2. Write the following tones in bass clef. Above each tone write another tone a major third higher.

    1) e♭¹ 2) c♯ 3) A 4) e 5) d♭¹
    6) a♭ 7) b 8) c♯¹ 9) D 10) f

3. Write the following tones in alto clef. Above each tone write another tone a minor sixth higher.

    1) c♯¹ 2) e♭ 3) f♯ 4) a♭ 5) g♭

4. Write the following tones in tenor clef. Above each tone write another tone a minor seventh higher.

    1) a♭ 2) c♯ 3) g♭ 4) b 5) e♯

5. Write the following tones in treble clef. Below each tone write another tone a perfect fifth below.

    1) a² 2) b¹ 3) g♯¹ 4) f² 5) d♭²
    6) c³ 7) e♯¹ 8) f♭² 9) a♭¹ 10) g♭¹

6. Write the following tones in bass clef. Below each tone write another tone a major sixth lower.

    1) B 2) f 3) a♯ 4) d♭¹ 5) c
    6) c♯¹ 7) f♯¹ 8) b♭ 9) e♭ 10) g♯¹

7. Write the following tones in alto clef. Below each tone write another tone an augmented second lower.

    1) f 2) b♭ 3) c♯¹ 4) d♭ 5) e¹

8. Write the following tones in tenor clef. Below each tone write another tone an augmented fourth below it.

    1) g 2) g♯¹ 3) c♯¹ 4) b♭ 5) f♯

9. Write the following harmonic intervals in the clef indicated. Use whole notes. Be careful to use the correct octave. (*A* means augmented; *M*, major; *m*, minor; and *d*, diminished. A2 should be read as augmented second, etc.)

A. *Treble Clef*
1) A2 above f♯♯²
2) A4 above d♭¹
3) d3 above c²
4) M6 above a
5) m2 above f¹
6) d5 above b♭
7) m7 above g♯¹
8) M3 above e♭¹
9) P4 above f
10) A3 above b♭¹
11) d6 above a♯¹
12) A5 above b
13) M7 above a♭¹
14) d7 above g♯
15) M2 below g♭²
16) m6 below a²
17) m3 below a♭¹
18) A6 below e²
19) P5 below b♭²
20) d4 below d♭²

B. *Bass Clef*
1) m7 above E♭
2) A5 above d
3) d6 above a♯
4) A3 above B♭
5) A4 above g♭
6) A2 above f
7) d7 above e♭
8) M2 above b
9) M6 above BB
10) d5 above e
11) m3 above d♭¹
12) M7 above G♭
13) P4 above F♯
14) d3 above g♯
15) m6 below e¹
16) d4 below a
17) m2 below c♭
18) P5 below d♯
19) A6 below c♯¹
20) M3 below A

C. *Alto Clef*
1) A5 above e♭
2) d3 above f♯¹
3) m7 above d♭¹
4) m6 above g♭¹
5) A2 above c♯
6) d5 above a♯
7) A4 above A
8) d7 below g¹
9) m2 below c♯¹
10) A6 below a♯¹

D. *Tenor Clef*
1) P4 above e
2) M2 above g♯
3) m3 above b
4) A6 above f
5) m7 above c
6) d5 above d¹
7) m6 above a♭
8) M3 below g♭¹
9) A2 below f¹
10) A4 below e♭¹

10. Copy the intervals in Figure 4.17 on manuscript paper; then write out the inversion of each of them. Name the given interval and the inverted interval.

Figure 4.17

5

Chords, the Basic
Units of Harmony

THE LAST CHAPTER was devoted to the interval, the aural relationship of only two musical pitches. Any collection of more than two harmonically related pitches, whether there be three, four, or more tones, is a *chord*. Any group of simultaneous tones may be called a chord provided the tones are related to each other, regardless of what their relationship is.

The chords that were used in the classic and romantic periods, roughly the eighteenth and nineteenth centuries, had a standardized structure heard and recognized by the relationship of each chord tone to a fundamental tone called the *root*. The root is the tone on which the chord is built. Other tones in the chord are at intervals of the third and fifth above the root; a few chords also have tones a seventh and a ninth above the root. Because the intervals between adjacent tones of these chords are thirds, chords having this structure are called *tertian chords*. The harmonic language that uses such chords is called *tertian harmony*. Music written prior to 1400, and some written after 1900, used chords that do not have a tertian structure; such music has *non-tertian harmony*. Only tertian harmony is discussed in this book.

Chords that have three different tones are called *triads;* those with four tones are *tetrads*. Similarly, chords having five, six, or seven different tones are *pentads*, *hexads*, or *heptads*. Most of the chords used in the eighteenth and nineteenth centuries were triads. When the three tones of a triad are played by more than three instruments, or sung by more than three voices, it is necessary to use some of the chord tones more than once. Sometimes the tones are doubled at the same pitch; at other times they are doubled at the octave or at two or more octaves. Each of the chords in Figure 5.1 is a tertian triad with doubled tones, copied exactly as it appears in a piece of music.

Figure 5.1. Tertian Triads

Figure 5.2 shows all the notes played by different instruments in a chord for full orchestra. Although there is much doubling, both at the unison and at various octaves, the chord consists of only three different notes: E♭, G, and B♭.

Figure 5.2. Doubled Tones in a Chord for Orchestra

Classic and romantic composers also used a few tetrads and some pentads. Chords with more than five tones were quite unusual during this period. With pentads and with tetrads, it was customary to omit one or more tones if there were only three or four instruments. Each of the chords in Figure 5.3 is a tertian chord with more than three tones, shown as it appears in a piece of music.

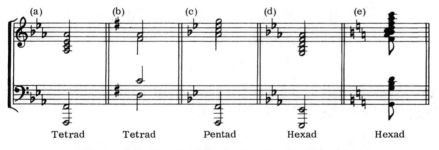

Figure 5.3. Tertian Tetrads, Pentads, and Hexads

All tertian triads consist of a *root*, a *third*, and a *fifth*. The qualities of the third and the fifth determine the *quality* of the triad. Four triad qualities have been used enough by composers to have recognized, well-established names. These four are the *major triad*, *minor triad*, *diminished triad*, and *augmented triad*. Each has a characteristic sound that a competent musician must be able to recognize and remember.

A *major triad* is composed of a root, and above that root the intervals of a major third and a perfect fifth, as in Figure 5.4.

CHORDS, THE BASIC UNITS OF HARMONY 59

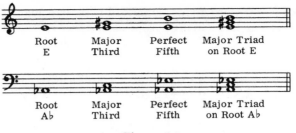

Figure 5.4

A *minor triad* is composed of a root, and above that root the intervals of a minor third and a perfect fifth, as in Figure 5.5.

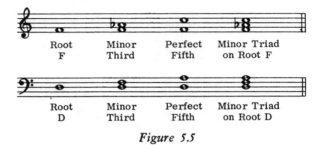

Figure 5.5

A *diminished triad* is composed of a root, and above that root the intervals of a minor third and a diminished fifth, as in Figure 5.6.

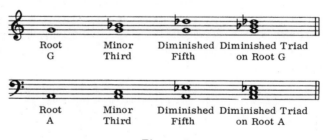

Figure 5.6

An *augmented triad* is composed of a root, and above that root the intervals of a major third and an augmented fifth, as in Figure 5.7.

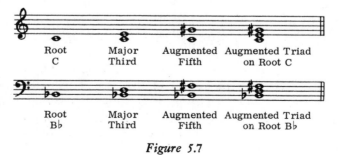

Figure 5.7

These four triads—major, minor, diminished, and augmented—are the only triads with established names. Other combinations of root, third, and fifth are possible, such as a major third and a diminished fifth, but none of these combinations has been used enough to acquire a name of its own.

ROOT/QUALITY ANALYSIS

One of the simplest means of analyzing tertian chords is a root/quality analysis. Although this is rudimentary and tells very little about the music as a whole, it will serve as a simple method of analysis for the time being. In a root/quality analysis, the root of the chord is written as the numerator of a fraction; and the chord quality, indicated by *M*, *m*, *d*, or *A*, for major, minor, diminished, or augmented, is written as the denominator. (A clear distinction must be made in writing M and m in order to avoid confusion.) The chords in Figure 5.8 have been analyzed in this way.

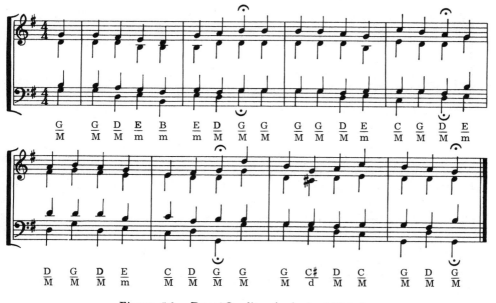

Figure 5.8. *Root/Quality Analysis of Triads*

INVERSIONS OF TRIADS

Although the structure of a tertian triad may always be reduced to root, third, and fifth, the tones may be arranged in any order desired. Any of the three tones may, under certain circumstances, be placed in the lowest part, called the *bass;* similarly, either root, third, or fifth may be in the highest part, called the *soprano.* The notes in between, called the *inner voices,* may also be arranged a number of different ways. If the root of the chord is the lowest sounding tone, the triad is in *root position.* If the bass has a tone other than the root, the triad is *inverted.* Each of the chords in Figure 5.9 is in root position, although the chords are differently spaced.

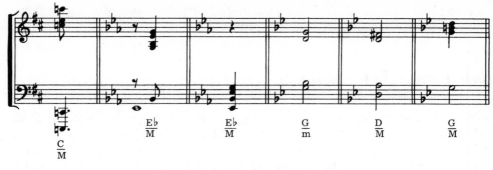

Figure 5.9. Triads in Root Position

If a triad is arranged so that the third of the chord is the lowest sounding tone, the triad is in *first inversion*. Each of the triads in Figure 5.10 is in first inversion.

Figure 5.10. Triads in First Inversion

If a triad is arranged so that the fifth of the chord is the lowest sounding tone, the triad is in *second inversion*. In classical harmony, second inversion chords were used only in particular circumstances, which will be discussed in Chapter 22. The triads in Figure 5.11 are all in second inversion.

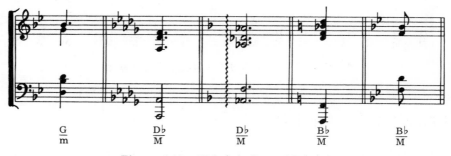

Figure 5.11. Triads in Second Inversion

To summarize:

1. A chord in root position has the root of the chord in the bass.

2. A chord in first inversion has the third of the chord in the bass.

3. A chord in second inversion has the fifth of the chord in the bass. (Second inversion chords are used only in special circumstances.)

SOPRANO POSITIONS OF CHORDS

The term *soprano position* refers to the highest note in the chord. A triad has three possible soprano positions. A chord with the root in the top voice is in the *position of the octave*. A chord with the third as the highest tone is in the *position of the third*. If the fifth of the triad is the highest tone, the chord is in the *position of the fifth*. Chords in different soprano positions are shown in Figure 5.12.

Figure 5.12. Chords in Different Soprano Positions

LEARNING THE SOUNDS OF TRIADS

A musician must learn the sounds, as well as the structures, of the four basic triads—major, minor, diminished, and augmented. He must be able not only to recognize the sound of each triad type, but also to reproduce it by singing each of the tones. The aural exercises at the end of this chapter will help to develop this skill. In singing triads, it is useful to call each chord member "root," "third," or "fifth," in order to associate the sound of each tone with its correct name.

ESSENTIAL VOCABULARY

1. chord
2. root
3. tertian chords
4. tertian harmony
5. non-tertian harmony
6. triad
7. tetrad
8. pentad
9. hexad
10. heptad
11. third
12. fifth
13. triad quality
14. major triad
15. minor triad
16. diminished triad
17. augmented triad
18. root/quality analysis
19. bass
20. soprano
21. inner voices
22. inverted triad
23. root position
24. first inversion
25. second inversion
26. soprano position
27. position of the octave
28. position of the third
29. position of the fifth

AURAL ASSIGNMENTS

The following exercises should be practiced regularly until skill in doing them is acquired.

1. Play any note on the piano; sing the major triad of which that note is the root. Repeat by playing other notes and singing the triad for each, as shown in Figure 5.13.

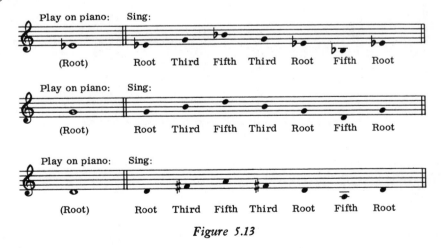

Figure 5.13

2. Repeat assignment No. 1 with minor triads.

3. Repeat assignment No. 1 with diminished and augmented triads.

4. Play any note on the piano; sing the major triad of which that note is the root. Play the same note again and sing the triad of which it is the third. Play the note a third time and sing the triad of which it is the fifth, as in Figure 5.14. Repeat, using other tones in the same way.

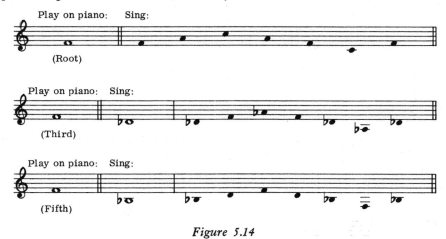

Figure 5.14

5. Repeat assignment No. 4 with minor triads.

6. Repeat assignment No. 4 with diminished and augmented triads.

7. Play any tone on the piano. Sing the major triad of which it is the root, first in root position, then in first inversion, and then in second inversion, as in Figure 5.15. When the range of the chord makes some notes difficult to sing, the triad may be transposed on octave higher or lower to make it more comfortable for the voice.

Figure 5.15

8. Repeat assignment No. 7 with minor triads.

9. Repeat assignment No. 7 with diminished and augmented triads.

WRITTEN ASSIGNMENTS

10. Spell the major triads on each of the following roots. Do not use a staff; be sure to use the proper accidentals.

a) D♭
b) F
c) A♯
d) C♭
e) E

f) G♯
g) F♯
h) B♭
i) A♭
j) D

11. Each of the following notes is the third of a major triad. Spell the triad without using a staff; be sure to use the proper accidentals.

a) C	f) D♭
b) E♯	g) E
c) A♭	h) F
d) C♭	i) G♯
e) B♯	j) A♯

12. Each of the following notes is the fifth of a major triad. Spell the triad without using a staff; be sure to use the proper accidentals.

a) B♭	f) A♯
b) D	g) E
c) C	h) G♯
d) F♯	i) B
e) D♭	j) F

13. Each of the following notes is the third of a minor triad. Spell the triad without using a staff; be sure to use the proper accidentals.

a) G♭	f) D♯
b) B♯	g) C
c) A♭	h) A
d) F♯	i) D♭
e) E♯	j) B

14. Each of the following notes is the fifth of a minor triad. Spell the triad without using a staff; be sure to use the proper accidentals.

a) D♭	f) B♯
b) C♭	g) A♯
c) G♭	h) G♯
d) E	i) B♭
e) F	j) D

15. Using the roots given below, write root position major triads as whole note chords on a staff, with a clef that will eliminate the need for ledger lines for any tone. Use no key signature, but take care to use the octave indicated.

a) e¹	i) g♭
b) G	j) b
c) g♯¹	k) e♭
d) B♭	l) b♭
e) f♯	m) b♭¹
f) c♭¹	n) d♯
g) a♭	o) d♯¹
h) c	

16. For each root and quality given below, write the proper triad as a whole note chord in the clef designated. Use any octave suited to the clef. Give a root/quality analysis, making a clear distinction between "M" and "m"; use no key signature.

A. *Treble Clef*

1. A♭ major	9. C dim.	17. A dim.
2. B♭ minor	10. D♭ major	18. C♯ aug.
3. E♭ aug.	11. A♯ major	19. G major
4. D♭ dim.	12. G♭ minor	20. A minor
5. C♯ major	13. F aug.	21. C aug.
6. E major	14. G dim.	22. B minor
7. F dim.	15. F♯ minor	23. G♭ dim.
8. D♯ minor	16. D major	24. D♯ major

B. *Bass Clef*

25. E♭ minor	33. C major	41. A♯ aug.
26. E aug.	34. B♭ aug.	42. G♭ major
27. G♭ aug.	35. D♭ minor	43. E dim.
28. A dim.	36. A♭ dim.	44. F♯ dim.
29. D minor	37. D♯ dim.	45. G♯ aug.
30. B minor	38. B♭ major	46. A♭ aug.
31. A major	39. E♭ dim.	47. G minor
32. D dim.	40. F major	48. A♯ minor

C. *Alto Clef*

49. C♯ dim.	54. A♭ minor
50. D aug.	55. B aug.
51. B♭ dim.	56. C♯ major
52. D♭ aug.	57. E minor
53. C minor	58. C♯ minor

D. *Tenor Clef*

59. A aug.	64. G♯ minor
60. G♯ dim.	65. G aug.
61. B major	66. F♯ major
62. F♯ aug.	67. D♯ aug.
63. F minor	68. E♭ major

17. Write a triad for each root, quality, inversion, and soprano position given below. Use only three notes for each chord, writing whole notes in the clef indicated. Give a root/quality analysis, making a clear distinction between "M" and "m"; use no key signature.

A. *Treble Clef*

ROOT	QUALITY	INVERSION	SOPRANO POS.
1. A♭	minor	first	octave
2. D♯	major	root pos.	fifth
3. C♯	aug.	root pos.	fifth
4. F	minor	second	third
5. B	major	first	octave
6. F♯	dim.	first	octave
7. E	minor	root pos.	fifth
8. G♭	major	root pos.	third
9. B♭	dim.	first	fifth
10. G♯	minor	second	third
11. F♯	major	root pos.	third
12. D♭	minor	second	third
13. E	dim.	first	octave
14. A	major	first	octave
15. B	minor	root pos.	third

B. *Bass Clef*

1. C♭	major	second	octave
2. A	minor	first	octave
3. B♭	aug.	first	fifth
4. A♯	minor	second	third
5. F	dim.	first	octave
6. F♯	major	root pos.	fifth
7. G	minor	root pos.	third

CHORDS, THE BASIC UNITS OF HARMONY

ROOT	QUALITY	INVERSION	SOPRANO POS.
8. D	dim.	first	fifth
9. D	major	root pos.	third
10. G	aug.	first	octave
11. C	major	root pos.	third
12. Eb	minor	root pos.	third
13. G♯	minor	second	octave
14. A	major	root pos.	third
15. Db	dim.	first	fifth

C. *Alto Clef*

ROOT	QUALITY	INVERSION	SOPRANO POS.
1. Gb	major	first	octave
2. D♯	dim.	first	fifth
3. Bb	minor	first	fifth
4. F♯	major	second	octave
5. C♯	minor	root pos.	third
6. G♯	dim.	first	octave
7. Eb	minor	root pos.	third
8. Ab	major	second	third
9. E	minor	root pos.	third
10. D	major	root pos.	fifth

D. *Tenor Clef*

ROOT	QUALITY	INVERSION	SOPRANO POS.
1. F	minor	root pos.	third
2. A♯	dim.	first	octave
3. G	major	second	octave
4. D♯	dim.	first	fifth
5. E	minor	root pos.	third
6. C♯	major	first	fifth
7. Db	minor	first	octave
8. Bb	major	root pos.	third
9. A	major	second	third
10. Gb	minor	root pos.	fifth

18. Make a root/quality analysis of the chords in the chorale in Figure 5.16. Write 1, 3, or 5 below each chord to show whether the root, third, or fifth of that chord is in the bass.

Figure 5.16

19. Make a root/quality analysis of the chords in the chorale in Figure 5.17. Indicate the soprano position of each chord by writing 3, 5, or 8 above the chord.

Figure 5.17

CHORDS, THE BASIC UNITS OF HARMONY 69

6

Tonality, Key, and Scales (Major)

EVERY PIECE OF music written in traditional style has one particular musical tone that is more important than others and is basic to the composition. This quality of one basic tone is called *tonality*. It is one factor that serves to unify a musical work.

Tonality may be established in a number of ways: for instance, the use of distinctive melodic patterns, the repetition of one tone more than others, or a rhythmic emphasis of one tone. Most of the concert and recital music heard today was written during the eighteenth and nineteenth centuries; it employs certain basic harmonic principles common to all the important composers who lived in that era.[1] In this common language, tonality is produced by a characteristic pattern of harmony. Melody helps establish tonality by implying certain chords. The use of one group of chords indicates one tonality; other chords indicate other tonalities. Tonality, in reference to the period of tertian harmony, is the result of the progression from one chord to another.

The basic pitch of the tonality is called the *keynote* or *tonic* (derived from the word "tone"). This tone is so important that it will normally be the root of the last chord of a piece of music. The chord having the keynote as its root is called the *tonic chord*. The tonality, however, is created, not by the tonic chord alone, nor by the keynote, but by the progression of chords, actual or implied, that leads to that final note or chord.

The ability of certain chords to establish tonality depends upon their relationship to each other. A chord is most significantly related to the chords whose roots are a perfect fifth above and a perfect fifth below its own root. Investigation has shown that the harmonic movement from one chord to another whose

---

[1] Among these were Bach, Handel, Haydn, Mozart, Beethoven, Schubert, Schumann, Mendelssohn, Brahms, Tchaikovsky, Wagner, Liszt, and Chopin.

root is a perfect fifth away was the most prevalent harmonic progression in the eighteenth century.[2]

Because of its great importance, the chord whose root is a perfect fifth above the tonic is called the *dominant chord*. The dominant chord may be a triad, tetrad, or even a pentad or hexad, but in any case, it has a tendency to move to, or, to use another term, *resolve* to the tonic chord. In most cases, the next to the last chord in a piece of music has a root that is a perfect fifth above the keynote or tonic. The chord whose root is a fifth below the tonic is also an important chord in any traditional tonality. Because its root is a perfect fifth lower than the tonic, this chord is called the *subdominant chord*. These three chords—the tonic, dominant, and subdominant—are called the *principal triads* of the tonality, because they are sufficient to establish that tonality without doubt.

MODE

In addition to a pitch, every tonality has an aural quality called *mode*. Throughout the history of music, quite a number of modes have been used; but in the eighteenth and nineteenth centuries, the period of common musical language with which we are concerned, only two modes were in common use—*major* and *minor*. Some of the more common modes other than major and minor are Dorian, Phrygian, pentatonic, and whole tone. Major mode will be discussed in this chapter; minor mode will be explained in Chapter 9. Other modes are beyond the scope of this book.

Mode represents the use of a particular pattern of tones, chosen from all the possible tones within an octave. The choice of tones may be affected by melodic or harmonic factors, or both. The musical result of the choice is an over-all sound, an aural quality that can be identified and distinguished from the sound of other modes. Thus major has a different sound from minor, and each of these is different from the sound of pentatonic or whole tone mode.

KEY

The concepts of both tonality and mode are combined in the term *key*. The name of a key states both the keynote and the mode. The key name G major, for instance, expresses both the tonality of G and the mode of that tonality.

SCALES

A musical *scale* is an arrangement in order of pitch of all the tones necessary to establish the tonality and mode of a piece of music. The scale customarily starts

---

[2] Allen I. McHose, *The Contrapuntal Harmonic Technique of the 18th Century.* New York: Appleton-Century-Crofts, Inc., 1947, p. 4.

with the keynote of the tonality. In major mode, the tones necessary to establish tonality and mode are the tones that make up the three principal triads—tonic, dominant, and subdominant. A major scale may then be constructed by merely arranging the tones of these triads in order of pitch. The tones obtained in this way are called the *diatonic tones* in that key.

If a major tonality is centered about the tone E♭, the three principal triads of the key will be those in Figure 6.1.

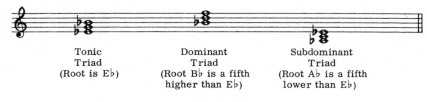

Tonic
Triad
(Root is E♭)

Dominant
Triad
(Root B♭ is a fifth
higher than E♭)

Subdominant
Triad
(Root A♭ is a fifth
lower than E♭)

Figure 6.1

The tones of these three major triads are:

Tonic	E♭	G	B♭
Dominant	B♭	D	F
Subdominant	A♭	C	E♭

If these diatonic tones are arranged in ascending order beginning with E♭, they would be:

E♭ F G A♭ B♭ C D E♭.

In musical notation, this would appear as in Figure 6.2.

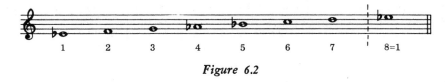

1   2   3   4   5   6   7   8=1

Figure 6.2

This series may be repeated octave after octave without change. Other diatonic major scales may be derived in the same manner, like Figure 6.3, for example:

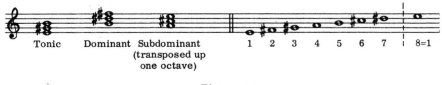

Tonic   Dominant Subdominant   1 2 3 4 5 6 7 8=1
                   (transposed up
                   one octave)

Figure 6.3

The tones of the diatonic scale are numbered upward, starting with the tonic. The seven tones that occur in any major scale have the following names, which must be memorized:

8 = 1	Tonic
7	Leading tone
6	Submediant
5	Dominant
4	Subdominant
3	Mediant
2	Supertonic
1	Tonic

MAJOR SCALE PATTERNS

Once the tones of any major scale have been determined from the principal triads and arranged in order, a fixed pattern of intervals may be discerned between those tones. Between the third and fourth tones (mediant and subdominant) and between the seventh and eighth tones (leading tone and tonic), there is a half step (minor second); between other adjacent tones, the interval is a whole step (major second). This pattern, shown in Figure 6.4, is characteristic of all major scales, regardless of what tone is used as the tonic.

Figure 6.4

KEY SIGNATURES IN MAJOR KEYS

Since it would be tedious to write accidentals before all the different notes that need them in some keys, it is customary to place the accidentals regularly used in a key all together in a *key signature* placed at the beginning of each staff of the music. If, for example, one examines the scale of B major as derived from its three principal triads, as in Figure 6.5, it will be seen that five sharped tones are used—C♯, D♯, F♯, G♯, and A♯. These five accidentals are arranged in a standard-

Figure 6.5

ized order to form the key signature for B major. Thus the scale may be more conveniently written in the form given in Figure 6.6. By a useful custom, the

TONALITY, KEY, AND SCALES (MAJOR)   73

Figure 6.6

accidentals are always written in the same order and in the same position on the staff. A key signature never has more than seven sharps or seven flats. The order of sharps from left to right is always:

F♯, C♯, G♯, D♯, A♯, E♯, B♯.

The sharps are always written in the positions shown in Figure 6.7; note that these positions vary in different clefs, since the identities of the lines and spaces

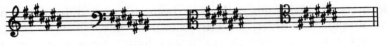

Figure 6.7

are of course different. The order of flats in the signature, from left to right, is always:

B♭, E♭, A♭, D♭, G♭, C♭, F♭.

Notice that the order of these letters is the reverse of that used for sharps. The flats are always written on the staff in the positions shown in Figure 6.8. The key

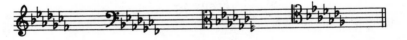

Figure 6.8

signatures for all of the major keys may be arranged in a diagram called the *circle of fifths*, shown in Illustration 6.1. Going clockwise around the circle, each key is successively a perfect fifth higher in pitch than the one before it. Going counterclockwise, each key is a perfect fifth lower. In all, there are fifteen major keys (including C major, which has no sharps or flats) that have signatures in common use. The signatures for these keys must be thoroughly memorized, much like the multiplication table.

Although key signatures are customarily shown in a circle like that in Illustration 6.1, the enharmonic change from sharps to flats at the bottom of the circle is valid only if instruments are tuned in equal temperament so that all half steps are exactly equal. In older tuning systems that are more acoustically perfect, but far less practical, the keys with sharps would continue indefinitely in a clockwise direction, and the keys with flats would continue in a counterclockwise direction. The result would not be a circle, but a never-ending spiral. It is just as impractical to continue the infinite succession of keys as it is to try to build keyboard instruments that have separate keys for F♯ and G♭ and for other enharmonic tones.

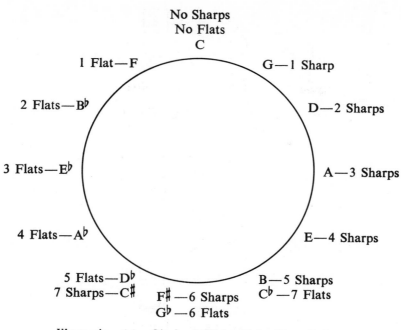

Illustration 6.1. Circle of Fifths, Major Keys Only

REST TONES AND TENDENCY TONES

The individual tones of the major scale may be divided into *rest tones* and *tendency tones* (active tones). The tones that make up the tonic triad are the tones that have a feeling of rest or inactivity; other tones exhibit melodic tendencies that require movement to one of the rest tones. The melodic tendencies of scale steps four and seven are quite strong, while steps two and six have weaker tendencies. Illustration 6.2 shows the tendency of each of the active tones.

The tendencies of the active tones may be stated briefly:

1. Two has a tendency to move to the tonic.

2. Four has a strong tendency to move to three.

3. Six has a tendency to move to five, but can easily be led to seven.

4. Seven has a very strong tendency to move to eight, giving rise to its name, *leading tone*.

The melodic tendency of each of the different steps of the major scale is analogous to a ball rolling on a hilly track, like that in Illustration 6.3. Such a ball would roll to a point of rest represented by scale step one, three, or five. At other scale steps, the ball would roll in the direction of the greater slopes.

TONALITY, KEY, AND SCALES (MAJOR)   75

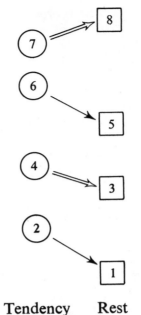

Tendency   Rest
  Tones   Tones

Illustration 6.2.   Melodic Tendencies of Tones in the Major Scale

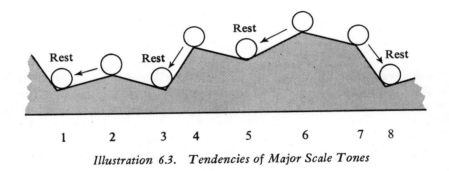

Illustration 6.3.   Tendencies of Major Scale Tones

LEARNING TO SING THE MAJOR SCALE

The sound of the major scale must be indelibly fastened in the mind of each music student. This is most easily done by constant practice in singing the scale tones, both in their regular order and in random order. The tones of the scale may be called by their numbers, or if students have previously used some other system of scale syllables (such as *do, re, mi,* etc.), that system may be employed.

Illustration 6.4 will be helpful in learning to sing the tones of the major scale. The diagram shows a column of numbers, each representing a tone in the major scale. The tonic triad has been emphasized by boxing the scale steps that are numbers of that chord. Two things should be especially helpful to the student—

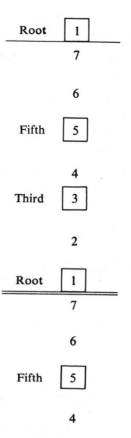

Tonic
Chord

Illustration 6.4. Tones of the Major Scale

the scale pattern represented by consecutive numbers, and the tonic chord pattern visible in the boxed numerals.

ESSENTIAL VOCABULARY

1. tonality
2. keynote
3. tonic
4. tonic chord
5. dominant
6. resolve
7. subdominant
8. principal triads
9. mode
10. key
11. scale

12. diatonic tones
13. leading tone
14. submediant
15. mediant
16. supertonic
17. major scale pattern
18. key signature
19. circle of fifths
20. rest tones
21. tendency tones

1. Discuss the difference between:
   a) root, bass, tonic
   b) tonality, mode, key, scale
   c) triad, chord, tetrad

2. Write the key signatures of C♭ major and C♯ major ten times each in treble clef and ten times each in bass clef.

3. Write out each of the following major scales without using a key signature. Indicate the pattern of whole and half steps for each scale.

B, C♭, F, G, A, D♭, E

4. Derive the key signatures for each of the following major keys by use of the three principal triads, as shown on page 72.

D, D♭, B♭, F♯, C♭, G♭, F

5. Determine the key signatures for each of the following major keys by building the scales from patterns of whole steps and half steps.

F♯, C♯, B♭, A♭, C, E♭, D

6. The numbers below refer to scale steps in the major key designated. Write these tones as whole notes in bass clef, using no key signature.

Sample:

Figure 6.9

Exercises:

1) 1, 4, 5, in F	14) 2, 3, 7, in D♭
2) 4, 1, 3, in D	15) 3, 6, 2, in F♯
3) 2, 4, 7, in A♭	16) 1, 7, 5, in G
4) 2, 6, 7, in F	17) 7, 3, 1, in C♭
5) 5, 7, 3, in B	18) 1, 5, 4, in G
6) 2, 3, 6, in C	19) 6, 4, 2, in C♯
7) 5, 7, 1, in C♭	20) 5, 7, 2, in F♯
8) 2, 4, 5, in C♯	21) 1, 6, 7, in D♭
9) 5, 4, 1, in G♭	22) 3, 4, 2, in F
10) 4, 5, 1, in E♭	23) 7, 5, 6, in E♭
11) 1, 5, 4, in E	24) 2, 6, 1, in E
12) 3, 6, 7, in B	25) 2, 4, 3, in A
13) 3, 2, 6, in A	26) 7, 4, 5, in B

7. Memorize the key signatures for all the major keys shown in Illustration 6.1.

7

Sight-Singing

A COMPETENT MUSICIAN should be able to look at a piece of music and know how it sounds without actually having to play the music on an instrument. If he is able to do this, he can read music, *i.e.*, he can hear, in his imagination, both the pitch and rhythm of the printed score.

The term *sight-reading* is often used to mean playing music without previous preparation. Although the ability to play music at sight is a useful skill, it is not the same as the ability to read, that is, to hear it silently. *Sight-singing* is the most common means of developing skill in reading music. Since the singer has no means of making a certain pitch except to think that pitch, singing reveals the degree to which the musician actually comprehends the written notation.

Proficiency in reading rhythmic patterns may be developed by using one of the counting procedures described in Chapter 3. Constant practice in reading rhythm is necessary to develop and maintain this skill. Most people learn to read the pitch of written music by a sense of *relative pitch*, which is the ability to imagine or produce other tones after one note of known pitch is played or sung. A sense of relative pitch is based on the recognition and recall of familiar patterns such as chords, scales, or even melody patterns. As the eye recognizes these familiar patterns in the score, the sounds are recreated in the mind of the musician. A very few persons have an inborn ability, called *absolute pitch*,[1] to remember pitches as independent, unrelated sounds. Recent research indicates that it is possible, but difficult to acquire this skill. It was formerly considered an inborn trait, which could not be consciously learned.

---

[1] *Pitch memory* and *pitch recognition* are more useful terms than *absolute pitch*. Pitch memory is the ability to remember the pitch of any note, and to reproduce that pitch by singing, humming, or whistling. Pitch recognition is the ability to name any note heard, without necessarily being able to produce the sound at any time.

METHODS OF SIGHT-SINGING

A number of methods are employed in teaching sight-singing. All of them have the same purpose—teaching the ability to read music. Although each method has its strong advocates, continued practice is more important than the choice of method. Students who sight-read enough will probably learn to read music regardless of method. Some procedures are based on learning to sing by absolute pitch, others by relative pitch. All the methods require some counting process for learning rhythm. Those requiring special syllables for different notes are called *solmization*[2] systems.

The Fixed-Do Method

The fixed-do method is the name given in the United States to the European *solfeggio* or *solfège*. In Romance languages, notes are called *do, re, mi, fa, sol, la,* and *si*,[3] instead of C, D, E, etc. Singing by the fixed-do system is the European equivalent of calling each note by its letter name. If accidentals occur, no change is made in the syllable name; the accidental is merely thought, and the pitch, of course, suitably altered. This procedure is illustrated in Figure 7.1.

European Names:	fa	la	la	re	mi	fa	mi	re
American Names:	F	A	A	D	E	F	E	D
Actual Pitch:	F♯	A	A	D	E	F♯	E	D

Figure 7.1. The Fixed-Do Method: Singing by Note Name

The Movable-Do Method

Sight-singing in many English and American schools is based on the syllables *do, re, mi, fa, sol, la,* and *ti,* which correspond to the notes of the major scale. The syllable *do* always represents the tonic, *re* the supertonic, and so on; the syllables represent different notes in different keys. In England this system, with some rhythmic notation added, is called *Tonic Sol-Fa;* it was developed there by Mr. J. Curwen, an English music publisher. In the southern United States, music is often published with the notes shaped to facilitate reading by syllable; each scale step in the key is represented by a different shape such as a square, a circle, a diamond, etc.

The method of singing by scale number differs from the movable-do method only in the syllables used. The tonic is called *one* instead of *do;* the supertonic is *two,* and so on. Figure 7.2 shows the procedure in singing by movable-do and by scale number.

---

[2] From the syllables *sol* and *mi,* often used in such sets of syllables.

[3] These syllables evolved from those first employed by Guido of Arezzo in the eleventh century—*ut, re, mi, fa, sol,* and *la. Do* later replaced *ut,* and *si* was added to provide a seventh tone.

	mi	sol	sol	do	re	mi	re	do
Movable Do:								
Scale Number:	3	5	5	1	2	3	2	1

Figure 7.2. The Movable-Do Method: Singing by Scale Step

Sight-Singing without Special Syllables

Sight-singing may also be accomplished without special syllables by keeping familiar chord and scale patterns in mind. In most of our music, melodies have a skeletal structure of chord tones, filled in with tones that are not a part of the harmony. Often the tones of the melody move by step from one to another, thus forming segments of one of the major or minor scales. The chord tones and scale segments thus form musical patterns that can be easily recognized and remembered. The way in which the melody tones may be thought is shown in Figure 7.3.

Figure 7.3. Sight-Singing by Familiar Patterns of Chord and Scale

The recognition of chord or scale patterns requires a visual span of several notes at one glance, not just of one or two notes at a time. Students must consciously force themselves to look at music, not in little pieces, like this:

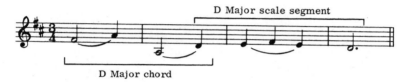

Illustration 7.1

but in large segments, like this:

Illustration 7.2

Within each span of vision, the sight reader must be able to recognize familiar patterns of chords or scales. A number of chord and scale patterns are shown in Figure 7.4. Complex melodies like the one at melody C sometimes involve tones that fit neither chord nor diatonic scale. These tones, called *non-harmonic tones*, are discussed in Chapters 13 and 21.

Sight-Singing by Interval

If one has memorized the sounds of all the common intervals, it is sometimes possible to sing by thinking "up a fourth," "down a second," "up a fifth," and so on. This procedure should be reserved for music that does not have a clearly established tonality, such as much modern music. It is probably the most difficult method of learning to read music.

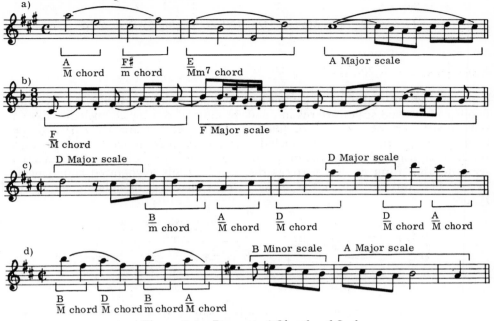

Figure 7.4. Patterns of Chord and Scale

SIGHT-SINGING SUGGESTIONS

By now it should be obvious that the ability to read music is a complex physical skill requiring the coordination of eye movement with the recognition of patterns of rhythm and pitch. All this must be done within the rhythmic beat of the music. The following suggestions will speed the process of learning to sight-sing.

1. *Keep your eyes moving ahead of where you are singing.* Only by looking ahead can the eyes grasp a segment of music large enough to be intelligible as a pattern or group. One cannot read in rhythm what has not already been seen. The end of the staff presents a special problem, for the eyes must move a long way back across the page to the beginning of the next staff. Training the eye to move in an easy sweeping motion is one of the more difficult problems in sight-singing. Sight-singing easy material at a fast tempo helps in learning to look ahead.

2. *Don't stop to correct mistakes.* If you make a mistake, keep going; try to sing the next notes correctly and in rhythm. Stopping disturbs both the sweeping motion of the eyes and the rhythm of the music. If you make too many errors, try easier material.

3. *Maintain a physical beat.* The beat should be regular and unvaried, like a metronome. It is best made with the hand, since foot tapping is noisy and might, by habit, be carried into an actual performance. Some people wiggle toes inside

their shoes. Physical movement in the irregular rhythm of the note values instead of a regular, metrical beat seems to be detrimental rather than helpful.

4. *Keep looking for recognizable patterns in the music.* Chord patterns, especially the tonic or dominant chords, and scale patterns are easily recognized groups. Principal tones in the key—tonic, dominant, and subdominant—are convenient points of reference.

5. *Read large quantities of easy material.* The music used for sight-singing should not be so difficult that it cannot be read in rhythm with few mistakes. If the rhythm of the music is disturbed by too many errors, easier material should be used.

Sight-singing is a skill that can be learned by almost anyone who will make diligent effort. It does not demand great musical talent. It is necessary, regardless of the method used, to read large quantities of easy material at a fast tempo. This trains the eyes in their proper, easy swinging motion, and also disciplines the musical mind in its recognition of pitches and rhythms. The ability to read music without an instrument is indispensable to any professional musician.

ESSENTIAL VOCABULARY

1. sight-reading
2. sight-singing
3. absolute pitch
4. pitch memory
5. pitch recognition
6. relative pitch
7. fixed-do
8. solfeggio
9. solfège
10. movable-do
11. Tonic Sol-Fa
12. solmization

8

Functions of Chords

in a Key

IN DISCUSSING TONALITY, key, and mode, the statement was made that in traditional harmony tonality or key was established by harmonic progression, that is, by the movement of chords, one to another. During the early part of the harmonic era in musical composition, the progression of chords developed a stable, well-defined pattern. Closely followed by almost all composers, the pattern of movement was analogous to a clearly understood musical grammar. In this grammatical system each chord within a key serves a particular function in relation to the tonal system, just as in the English language, some words are nouns, others verbs, and still others prepositions, adjectives, and so on. This harmonic language is called *functional harmony*.

FUNCTIONAL ANALYSIS

In analyzing the structure of a language it is useful to have names for the parts of speech; in music, a similar purpose is fulfilled by naming chords according to their function within the prevailing key. The root/quality analysis described in Chapter 5 does not serve this purpose, because it is independent of key. A more useful analysis assigns each chord in a key the name of the scale step that serves as root of the chord. This is commonly done by writing Roman numerals for chord names, as shown in Figure 8.1. The chord whose root is the supertonic, for instance, is a II chord (two chord); one whose root is the dominant is the V chord (five chord). Stating the key is extremely important in functional analysis, because the same chord may have different functions in each of several keys.

Although some people use capital letters for major keys and lower-case letters for minor keys, much confusion can be avoided by stating the key in full, as E major, Bb major, Bb minor, F# major, etc.

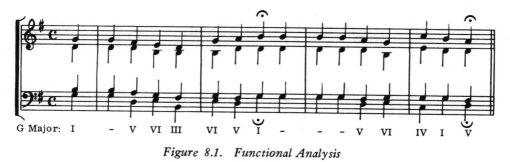

G Major: I   -   V VI III   VI V I   -   -   - V VI   IV I V

Figure 8.1.   Functional Analysis

Before discussing the system of functional harmony in more detail, let us briefly review the vocabulary of diatonic chords in a major key. The name and quality of each chord in Figure 8.2 should be carefully studied. Note that there are three major chords (I, IV, V), three minor chords (II, III, VI), and one diminished triad (VII). Chords with identical functions have the same quality in all major keys; the II chord is a minor triad in all major keys, for instance.

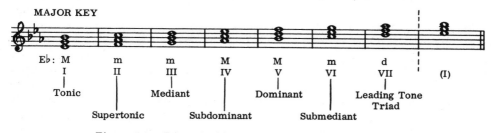

Figure 8.2.   Diatonic Chord Vocabulary in Major Mode

BASIC CHORD PROGRESSIONS

The importance of the interval of the perfect fifth in western music has already been mentioned in the discussion of the dominant and subdominant triads. The basic progression of chords is another example of the importance of this interval. The natural movement of a chord is to another chord whose root is a perfect fifth lower (or by inversion a perfect fourth higher) than its own. Because this is the most frequent of all chord progressions, the movement of chords whose roots descend a perfect fifth is called the *primary resolution* of a chord. Examples of primary resolution include V to I, II to V, VI to II, and III to VI.

Of the other progressions that may occur, the most common is the *secondary resolution*, in which the roots move upward through the interval of a second. This resolution is the second most frequent chord progression. In its primary resolution, the subdominant would resolve to an unstable diminished triad. Since this is usually undesirable, a secondary resolution to the dominant is more often used; this is a root movement of an upward second. In a comparable situation, the leading tone triad, which has a close affinity for the tonic, moves more frequently by secondary than by primary resolution. Other common secondary resolutions include the movements III to IV and V to VI.

A less frequent chord progression involves root movement through the interval of a third, either upward or downward; such a progression is called *third relationship*. Although not used as often as the primary and secondary resolutions, it is by no means uncommon, especially during and after the time of Beethoven and Schubert. Frequent chord progressions using third relationship include: I to III, I to VI, VI to IV, and IV to II.

Any chord progression other than the three already described may be considered an *irregular resolution*. Root movement down a second or down a fourth would fall in this category.

CHORD PROGRESSION WITHIN A MAJOR KEY

Within the framework of a given key or tonality, functional harmony operates in an organized pattern of chord movement. Each chord, because of its relation to the tonic, serves a particular function within the key. The most frequent chord in traditional harmony is the tonic, and the movement of the other chords may be compared to a gravitational system in which the tonic chord is the lowest level toward which all other chords move. The tonic chord functions differently from other chords by virtue of its having the keynote as its root; it is essentially a point of harmonic rest. Unlike other chords within a key system, the tonic does not utilize its basic primary or secondary resolution; it moves freely to any other chord within the key, a privilege not shared by the other chords.

Chords other than the tonic operate at different harmonic levels, depending upon the number of progressions usually needed to reach the tonic. Chords that reach the tonic by one harmonic movement are at the first level; those that require two progressions are at the second level; and so on. Illustration 8.1 shows the harmonic levels of the diatonic chords in major mode.

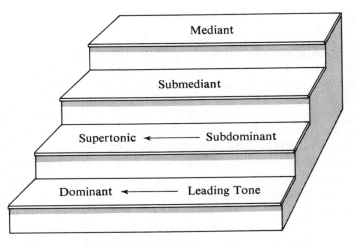

Illustration 8.1.   *Harmonic Levels of Diatonic Chords in Major Keys*

The dominant and leading tone triads are at the first level, one step away from the tonic. The supertonic and subdominant chords are at the next level, two harmonic steps from the tonic. The submediant is at level three, and the mediant at level four. Tonic tetrads (which will be explained in Chapter 11) are at level three; other tetrads have the same position as their corresponding triads.

The dominant and leading tone chords, which are one harmonic step above the tonic, move to the tonic by primary and secondary resolutions respectively. A close look will reveal that change from one harmonic level to another is most easily made by a primary resolution, which is the most frequent harmonic progression. If two chords are at the same harmonic level, a progression from one to the other is usually in the direction of the chord that moves toward the tonic by a primary resolution. Such movement is indicated by the arrows in Illustration 8.1.

A progression of chords is usually from the tonic to some other chord in the key, and then back step by step to the tonic. Chord progressions other than this, either in the direction of the tonic or away from the tonic, occur less frequently. Harmonic progression that does not follow step-by-step downward movement to the tonic is used to vary the regular pattern. Any unusual progression should be examined to see if it is a secondary resolution, third relationship, or an irregular resolution.

ESSENTIAL VOCABULARY

1. functional harmony
2. functional analysis
3. primary resolution
4. secondary resoluton
5. third relationship
6. irregular resolution
7. harmonic level
8. harmonic step

ASSIGNMENTS

1. Write the chords designated below in whole notes in the proper clef. Use no key signature, but employ the proper accidentals for each chord. Each key represented is a major key. Below each chord write its functional analysis (*be sure to state the key*) and its root/quality analysis. These chords do not represent chord progressions, but are separate chords.

A. *Treble Clef*

1) Ab: I, VII, IV
2) F: II, VI, III
3) Gb: IV, I, VII
4) C: V, VII, I
5) Db: I, II, V
6) C#: V, IV, VI
7) B: VII, VI, II
8) Cb: III, IV, VI
9) A: II, III, V
10) G: VI, III, V
11) E: II, VI, I
12) Eb: V, IV, I

B. *Bass Clef*

1) F#: VI, I, III
2) Bb: I, VII, II
3) D: V, VII, II
4) C: VII, IV, V
5) Gb: VI, III, II
6) C#: VII, I, IV

7) B: V, VI, IV   10) E♭: II, VI, III
8) F: IV, VI, II   11) F♯: VII, I, V
9) A: III, VII, IV   12) A♭: VI, IV, I

C. *Alto Clef*

1) D♭: VII, I, III   4) E: V, IV, VII
2) B♭: VI, III, VII   5) C♭: II, VI, V
3) D: IV, I, II

D. *Tenor Clef*

1) E♭: III, V, I   4) F♯: IV, II, V
2) G: I, II, VII   5) A♭: I, VII, III
3) C: III, V, VI

2. Copy the examples in Figure 8.4. Make a functional analysis of each chord and indicate the harmonic level of each, as shown in the sample exercise.

Sample:

A Major: I   –   –   –   V   –   I   V   I   IV   I   V
       Tonic   1st   Tonic   1st   Tonic   2nd   Tonic   1st
                           Level   Level   Level   Level

Figure 8.3

Exercises:

a)

b)

c)

d)

Figure 8.4

9

Tonality, Key, and Scales (Minor)

I<small>N</small> T<small>HE</small> D<small>ISCUSSION</small> of major scales in Chapter 6, it was shown that if the tones of the three principal major triads—tonic, dominant, and subdominant—were arranged in order, they would form the major scale for that key. Minor keys, however, do not show this same consistency. Over a period of some centuries, minor mode evolved in such a way that some of its tones have dual forms, one form or the other being used according to the circumstances. The source of these variable tones is in the modal usage of the Middle Ages, especially the mode known as Aeolian mode. Even today, minor keys use the same signature that would be employed for this mode.

KEY SIGNATURES IN MINOR KEYS

The key signature in minor keys is derived from three principal minor triads—the minor triads on the tonic, dominant, and subdominant. If, for example, the tonality is F and the aural quality is minor, the three principal minor triads will be those in Figure 9.1.

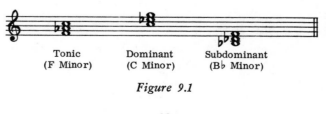

Tonic   Dominant   Subdominant
(F Minor)   (C Minor)   (B♭ Minor)

Figure 9.1

The tones of these three minor triads are:

Tonic:	F, A♭, C
Dominant:	C, E♭, G
Subdominant:	B♭, D♭, F

In order of pitch, these tones would be:

F, G, A♭, B♭, C, D♭, E♭

In musical notation, the scale of F minor could then be written in musical notation like Figure 9.2.

Figure 9.2

This may be rewritten with a key signature, in the form shown in Figure 9.3.

Figure 9.3

The key signature for each minor key is derived from the accidentals needed for the three minor triads on the tonic, dominant, and subdominant roots. The key signature of C♯ minor, to cite the example in Figure 9.4, consists of those accidentals needed to form the three principal minor triads.

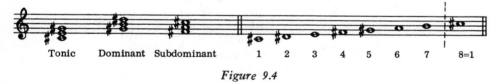

Figure 9.4

Since four sharps are needed, these may be written more conveniently as a key signature, as in Figure 9.5, just as was done with major key signatures or with the key of F minor described above.

Figure 9.5

The tones of the three triads form a scale known as the *natural minor scale*. The natural minor scale is useful for determining key signatures in minor mode, but it is rarely used in actual music.

The sharps or flats needed for minor signatures are written on the staff in exactly the same order used for major signatures. There are fifteen minor keys; their signatures should be thoroughly memorized.

TONALITY, KEY, AND SCALES (MINOR)

PARALLEL AND RELATIVE KEYS

Major and minor keys that have the same tonic note are called *parallel* keys; C minor is therefore parallel to C major, and vice versa. Major and minor keys that have different tonic notes but use the same key signature are known as *relative* keys. The tonic of a minor key is always a minor third lower than that of its relative major key. The key of D minor is the relative minor of F major; F major is the relative major of D minor.

The circle of fifths may now be revised, as shown in Illustration 9.1, to include minor as well as major keys. It is customary to show major keys outside the circle, and minor keys with the same signature inside the circle.

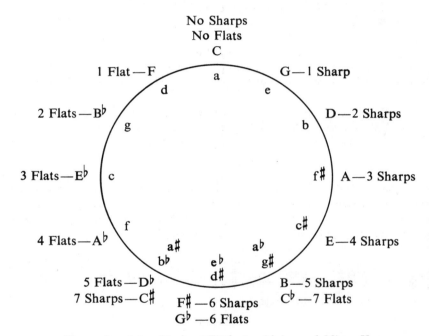

Illustration 9.1.   Circle of Fifths for Major and Minor Keys

ALTERNATE TONES IN THE MINOR SCALE

Although the natural minor scale is useful to us in that it determines the customary key signature for each of the minor keys, this scale does not contain all the tones that are regularly used in a minor mode. Three tones in minor keys—the third, sixth, and seventh scale steps—have developed dual or alternate forms. One form is that called for by the signature; the other is indicated by an accidental whenever it is needed. Because both forms of these three tones are essential in minor mode, they are considered to be diatonic tones in a minor key.

The seventh scale step in natural minor does not move to the tonic in a way that convincingly establishes a feeling of conclusion or finality. As early as the fourteenth century, musicians began to alter the modes they used so that the seventh scale step was only one half step instead of a whole step below the tonic. This usage has remained as a part of minor mode. The seventh scale step thus has two forms—the unaltered one required by the key signature, and a raised form indicated by an accidental.

The sixth scale step also has a raised form as well as that indicated by the key signature. The raised form in this case developed as a means of avoiding the awkward interval that occurred between the raised seventh scale step and the unaltered sixth step.

The other variable note in minor mode is the third scale step. Composers of the sixteenth and seventeenth centuries were reluctant to employ a minor triad for the last chord of a piece of music, so they raised the third of the last chord, making it a major triad. The raised third step was known as a *Picardy third;* it was used only in the final chord of a piece of music, or in the last chord of a large section of a composition.

If one includes both the altered and unaltered forms of the three variable tones, the minor scale takes the form seen in Figure 9.6, known as the *composite minor scale* or the *ten-tone minor scale.*[1]

Figure 9.6

The tones of the minor scale are listed in Table 9.1. The names given must be memorized.

---

[1] Music theorists often mention the *harmonic minor* and *melodic minor* scales. Although these terms do not extend our understanding of the minor mode beyond what can be gained from the composite minor scale, they are used so widely that students should know what the terms mean. Harmonic minor has one alteration; in it the leading tone is always used instead of the subtonic, as shown in Figure 9.7.

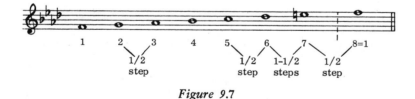

Figure 9.7

Melodic minor, Figure 9.8, has an ascending form in which the sixth and seventh steps are both raised by accidentals and a descending form that is identical with natural minor. The words *ascending* and *descending* in this context refer to whether the sixth and seventh scale steps are followed by higher or lower notes, not to the way they are approached, nor to the general upward or downward motion of the melodic line.

Figure 9.8

TONALITY, KEY, AND SCALES (MINOR)

Table 9.1. Tones of the Minor Scale

8 = 1	Tonic
7 (raised)	Leading tone
7 (unaltered)	Subtonic
6 (raised)	Dorian sixth (also called raised submediant)
6 (unaltered)	Submediant
5	Dominant
4	Subdominant
3 (raised)	Picardy third
3 (unaltered)	Mediant
2	Supertonic
1	Tonic

The alternate forms of the third, sixth, and seventh scale steps are used under the following specific circumstances:

1. *Seventh Scale Step.* Where harmonic considerations are of primary concern, the leading tone is used whenever the seventh scale step is a part of a chord in the first harmonic level above the tonic. (See Chapters 8 and 10.) If melody is the primary concern, the leading tone is used at all times, except when the seventh scale step is followed by the unaltered sixth scale step in the same *voice*.[2]

2. *Sixth Scale Step.* The submediant in minor is the normal form. The Dorian sixth (raised submediant) is used only when the sixth scale step is followed by the leading tone (the raised seventh scale step) in the same voice.

3. *Third Scale Step.* The mediant in minor is the normal form. The Picardy third is used only when it is desirable to make the last chord of a piece, or of a large section of a piece, major.

Two excerpts from Bach chorales show the use of these altered tones in minor mode. In Figure 9.9, which is in the key of A minor, the leading tone, G♯, occurs each time the seventh step appears except in the bass voice, in which G natural, the subtonic, is followed by F natural, the unaltered submediant.

Bach

Christus, der uns selig macht

Figure 9.9. Use of Altered Tones in Minor Mode

Figure 9.10 is actually in the key of C minor, in spite of Bach's use of only two flats in the signature. The A natural in the bass is a Dorian sixth, necessitated by the leading tone which follows. Since the key signature is irregular, there is no

---

[2] The word *voice* refers to any specific part, whether vocal or instrumental, such as tenor or viola. In keyboard music, the term refers to a single continuous melodic line, which may be only part of the total musical fabric.

accidental before the Dorian sixth. In this example, each use of the seventh scale step employs the leading tone, B natural.

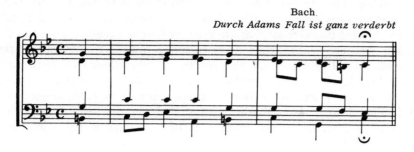

Figure 9.10.   *Another Use of Altered Tones in Minor Mode*

REST TONES AND TENDENCY TONES IN THE MINOR SCALE

The tones in the minor scale have melodic tendencies similar to those of the scale tones in major; some differences develop, however, because of the variable steps in the minor scale. As in major, all the tones of the tonic triad, including the

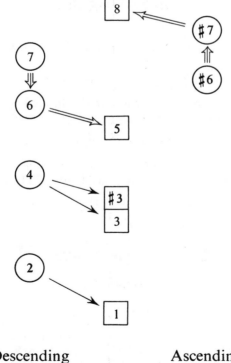

Descending Tendency Tones   Rest Tones   Ascending Tendency Tones

Illustration 9.2.   *Tendency Tones in Minor Mode*

Picardy third when it is used, are rest tones. The second and fourth scale steps, having no variable forms, have the same tendencies as their corresponding tones in major mode. The second scale step tends to move downward to the tonic; the fourth scale step has a strong tendency to move downward to the third scale step.

Of the variable tones, those that are unaltered have a tendency to move downward. The unaltered submediant tends to move toward the dominant; the subtonic tends to move down to the unaltered submediant. In both cases the downward tendency is much stronger than with their major counterparts.

The raised sixth and seventh scale steps have strong tendencies to move upward. The Dorian sixth almost always leads to the leading tone, and the leading tone to the tonic. The tendencies of the tones in the minor scale are shown in Illustration 9.2.

ESSENTIAL VOCABULARY

1. natural minor scale
2. parallel keys
3. relative keys
4. Picardy third
5. composite minor scale
6. ten-tone minor scale
7. Dorian sixth
8. subtonic
9. voice

ASSIGNMENTS

1. Write out the following minor scales in their natural forms without using key signatures:

F, C♯, G, E, G♯, D, B♭

2. Derive the key signatures for each of the following minor keys by use of the three principal triads, as shown on page 90:

B, F♯, E♭, G, D, C♯, B♭

3. The numbers below refer to scale steps in the minor keys designated. Write these tones as whole notes in treble clef, like Figure 9.11, using no key signature.

Sample:

1, 5, ♯7, in b.

Figure 9.11

Exercises:

1) 3, 5, 1, in D
2) ♯3, ♯7, 2 in G♯
3) 5, 3, ♯7, in E♭
4) 4, 1, ♯7, in C
5) 6, 4, 1, in F♯
6) 4, 3, 2, in A
7) ♯6, 7, 4, in B♭
8) ♯6, ♯7, 6, in F
9) 6, 1, 5, in G
10) 2, 3, 6, in C♯
11) 1, 3, 7, in B
12) 2, 3, ♯7, in D♯

13) ♯7, 3, 5, in A♯   20) 5, 4, 3, in C♯
14) 6, ♯3, 4, in E   21) 3, 5, 2, in B
15) 4, 6, ♯7, in A♭   22) 3, ♯7, ♯6, in G
16) 1, 4, 6, in E   23) ♯7, 4, 3, in B♭
17) 1, 5, 2, in D♯   24) 4, 1, 6, in F♯
18) 1, ♯7, 2, in A♯   25) ♯6, 1, 2, in F
19) 5, ♯6, 6, in A♭   26) 3, 7, 6, in D

4. The chorale excerpt in Figure 9.12 is in the key of B minor. Change any accidentals necessary so that alternate tones are used according to the principles stated on page 94. Check all four voices.

Figure 9.12

5. Memorize the key signatures for all the major and minor keys shown in Illustration 9.1.

10

Chords Within
a Minor Key

THE INTERRELATIONSHIP OF chords within a minor key is quite like that in major keys. The chord vocabulary is larger, however, because of the variable tones in the minor scale. These variable tones must be shown in a functional analysis, since they do affect the harmonic levels of the chords involved.

FUNCTIONAL ANALYSIS IN MINOR KEYS

As with major keys, chords in minor keys are assigned the name of the scale step that serves as the root of the chord. A Roman numeral in the functional analysis indicates a chord built of the tones in the natural minor scale as indicated by the key signature. If one of the variable tones is altered from natural minor, such an alteration must be shown in the analysis. The most common method of indicating the alteration is the use of either a sharp or a flat, and an Arabic numeral to indicate the scale step that has been changed, as shown in Figure 10.1. The symbol V is read "five, sharp seven" and indicates a chord on a dominant root in $\overset{\sharp}{7}$ which the seventh scale step (the third of the chord) has been raised one half step from the signature of the existing key. The chord IV, read "four, sharp six," $\overset{\sharp}{6}$ has a similar meaning.

G Minor: V   V   IV   IV
                     #   #
                     7   6

Figure 10.1. Indicating Altered Tones in a Functional Analysis

The sharp or flat, so used, means only that the scale step in question has been raised or lowered, not that the tone must literally have a sharp or flat before it in the music. Figure 10.2 shows two excerpts, each with both a functional analysis and a root/quality analysis. Note that in the excerpt in C minor, Figure 10.2a, there is a a sharp and a seven in the analysis, which refer to a B natural in the music.

Figure 10.2. Functional Analysis in Minor Keys

Let us now look briefly at the vocabulary of chords in a minor key. Although some of these chords contain tones not called for by the key signature, such altered forms are used regularly and therefore form an essential part of the minor vocabulary. These altered forms, because they are a part of the regular vocabulary, are called *diatonic alterations*. Figure 10.3 includes all the diatonic chords in minor mode. As with major mode, chords having the same functional analysis will have the same quality in all minor keys. The II chord is a minor triad in

any minor key; V is a major triad in any minor key.

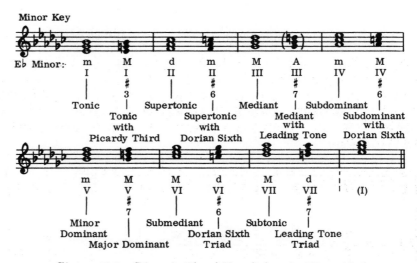

Figure 10.3. Diatonic Chord Vocabulary in Minor Mode

BASIC CHORD PROGRESSIONS

Chords in minor mode have the same basic progressions as those in major—the primary resolution with downward root movement of a perfect fifth, the secondary resolution with upward root movement of a second, and third relationship, with root movement of a third in either direction. It is only when the variable tones of the minor scale are involved that chord progression differs from major mode.

CHORD PROGRESSION WITHIN A MINOR KEY SYSTEM

The tonic in minor, as in major, is the point of rest toward which all other chords move as if by gravity. The tonic chord can move freely to any other chord in the key, without regard for its primary resolution, secondary resolution, and so on. The remaining chords are at different harmonic levels, depending upon the number of harmonic progressions needed to reach the tonic. One step away, at the first level, are the major dominant chord and the leading tone chord. All forms of the supertonic and subdominant chords are at the second level. The third level includes the submediant and the minor form of the dominant triad.

The mediant triad (a major triad) is at the fourth level, and the subtonic is at the fifth.

Illustration 10.1 shows the harmonic levels of chords in both major and minor mode. In order for the illustration to be complete for later reference, some chords have been included that have not yet been studied.

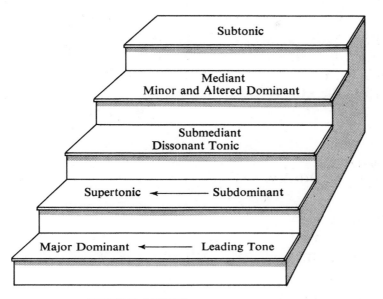

TONIC LEVEL

Illustration 10.1. Harmonic Levels of Chords

ASSIGNMENTS

1. Write the chords designated below in whole notes in the proper clef. Use no key signature, but write in the proper accidentals for each chord. Each key is a minor key. Below each chord write its functional analysis (*be sure to state the key*) and its root/quality analysis. These chords do not represent chord progressions, but separate chords.

A. *Treble Clef*

1) A♯: II, III, I

2) D♯: VII, V, IV
   ♯7 ♯7

3) E: V, VII, IV
   ♯7

4) B: VII, II, V
   ♯7   ♯7

5) A♭: III, I, VI

6) D: I, III, IV
   ♯6

7) G♯: II, VI, IV
   ♯6

8) G: VI, VII, I
   ♯7 ♯3

9) F: VI, II, V
   ♯6 ♯7

10) C♯: V, VI, V
    ♯7

11) F♯: III, VII, IV

12) E♭: III, VII, I
    ♯7

B. *Bass Clef*

1) Ab: VI, II, V
7) F#: VI, III, VII

#/7 (under VII)

2) Eb: V, IV, VII

#/7, #/6, #/7

8) C: II, III, I

#/6 (under I)

3) A: V, IV, VI

#/7 (under V)

9) D: III, VI, I

4) Bb: V, II, I

#/7, #/3

10) E: II, IV, VII

#/7 (under VII)

5) F: II, I, V

11) G#: II, IV, II

#/6 (under last II)

6) F#: III, VII, VI

#/7 (under VII)

12) B: VI, II, V

#/7 (under V)

C. *Alto Clef*

1) A: VII, III, VI

#/7, #/7

2) D#: I, V, IV

#/7, #/6

3) Ab: V, III, II

#/7 (under V)

4) Bb: II, VII, III

#/6, #/7

5) A#: V, VII, I

#/7 (under VII)

D. *Tenor Clef*

1) G: I, II, VI
2) C#: I, IV, VI
3) F: I, VI, V

#/3, #/7

4) Eb: IV, II, III
5) B: II, VI, VII

2. Copy the musical examples in Figure 10.4. Make a functional analysis of each chord and indicate the harmonic level of each.

a)

Figure 10.4

11

Chords of More
Than Three Tones

Tᴇᴛʀᴀᴅꜱ, ALTHOUGH NOT as frequent as triads, also play an important role in tertian harmony. Tetrads are formed by adding an extra tone to a triad, making a chord of four tones. A tertian tetrad, or *seventh chord*, consists of a root, and above that root the intervals of the third, fifth, and seventh. In traditional harmony, tetrads, pentads, and higher-order chords are always considered to be dissonant, meaning that they have to move to another chord; they thus require a chord of resolution to follow them. Use the term *seventh* only to mean 1) the interval of a seventh, or 2) the seventh of a chord. Do not use it to mean the seventh tone in a scale; this should be called either *leading tone* or *subtonic*. When writing traditional harmony, the seventh of any tetrad is approached smoothly. It is left by downward step to one of the tones in the following chord.

SEVENTH CHORDS

Tetrads, like triads, differ in aural quality. Since there are more tones in this chord than in the triad, there are greater possibilities for differences in sound. The quality of a seventh chord is described by 1) naming the quality of the triad on which it is built, and 2) stating the quality of the interval of the seventh above the chord root. A major triad with a minor seventh above its root is called a *major-minor seventh chord*. The structure of the established tetrads, as well as the four basic triads, may be found in Table 11.1.

Table 11.1. Structure of Tertian Triads and Tetrads

TRIADS

QUALITY SYMBOL	FULL NAME	CONSTRUCTION
M	Major triad	Root + major third + perfect fifth
m	Minor triad	Root + minor third + perfect fifth
d	Diminished triad	Root + minor third + diminished fifth
A	Augmented triad	Root + major third + augmented fifth

TETRADS

QUALITY SYMBOL	FULL NAME	CONSTRUCTION	ALSO CALLED
Mm^7	Major-minor seventh chord	Major triad + minor seventh	Dominant seventh
MM^7	Major-major seventh chord	Major triad + major seventh	
mm^7	Minor-minor seventh chord	Minor triad + minor seventh	Minor seventh
mM^7	Minor-major seventh chord	Minor triad + major seventh	
dm^7	Diminished-minor seventh chord	Diminished triad + minor seventh	Half-diminished seventh
$dd^7 (d^7)$	Diminished-diminished seventh chord	Diminished triad + diminished seventh	Diminished seventh
Am^7	Augmented-minor seventh chord	Augmented triad + minor seventh	

The most important single tetrad, the *dominant seventh chord*, is the major-minor seventh chord whose root is the dominant tone of the key. Other tetrads are called *secondary seventh chords;* they occur less frequently than the dominant seventh.

Inversions of Seventh Chords

Since a tetrad has one more tone than a triad, there are three inverted forms rather than two. The definitions of root position, first inversion, and second inversion, given on pages 61 and 62, are the same for seventh chords as for triads. A tetrad is in *third inversion* if the seventh of the chord is the lowest sounding tone. In similar fashion, a tetrad also has another soprano position, the *position of the seventh*. The chords in Figure 11.1 show different inversions and soprano positions for the major-minor seventh chord.

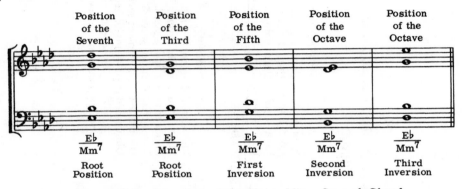

Figure 11.1. *Inversions of the Major-Minor Seventh Chord*

FUNCTIONAL ANALYSIS OF TETRADS

The functional analysis of seventh chords is like that of triads, except that an Arabic superscript number seven (7) is placed after the Roman numeral to show that the chord contains a seventh. Altered tones are indicated just as they are with triads. Figure 11.2 shows the functional analysis of two phrases containing seventh chords, one in C major and one in G minor.

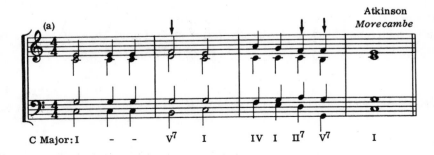

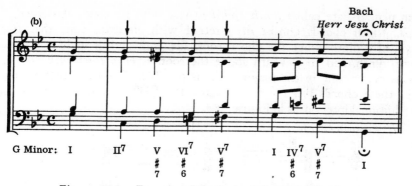

Figure 11.2. *Functional Analysis of Seventh Chords*

In a major key, the seventh chords on each of the tones of the scale have the qualities shown in Figure 11.3.

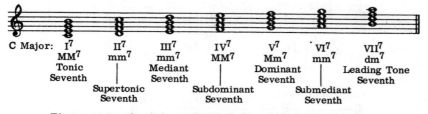

Figure 11.3. *Qualities of Seventh Chords in Major Mode*

The qualities of the seventh chords in minor keys are shown in Figure 11.4.

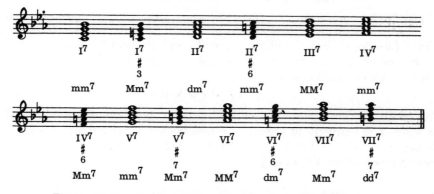

Figure 11.4. *Qualities of Seventh Chords in Minor Mode*

The seventh chords listed above are those that have been used enough to make them a part of our standard harmonic vocabulary. It is possible to construct other seventh chords for which composers have found little or no use, just as certain combinations of letters have never found their way into our language as words.

CHORDS WITH MORE THAN FOUR TONES

Although triads and tetrads make up the bulk of traditional harmony, chords of five, six, or even seven tones sometimes occur. Tertian chords of five tones, tertian pentads, are called *ninth chords;* those with six tones are called *eleventh chords.* Ninth chords consist of a tetrad with an extra tone that forms the interval of a ninth above the chord root. Eleventh chords include a third, fifth, seventh, ninth, and an eleventh above the root. Even a *thirteenth chord,* which contains every tone in the major scale, is possible. The root/quality analysis of any of these chords just mentioned states the quality of the triad, then that of each additional interval, as in Figure 11.5.

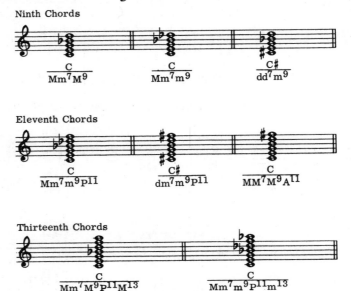

Figure 11.5. *Root/Quality Analysis of Ninth, Eleventh, and Thirteenth Chords*

In a functional analysis, ninth, eleventh, and thirteenth chords are indicated by an Arabic superscript next to the chord function, following the same procedure as with seventh chords:

$$V, V^7, V^9, V^{11}, V^{13}$$

Most ninth, eleventh, and thirteenth chords are built on the dominant tone of the scale. The harmony in Figure 11.6 uses both a V^9 chord and a VI^7 chord in the key of E major. (What appears to be a D♯/dd⁷ chord on beat two is really a continuation of the V^9 chord.)

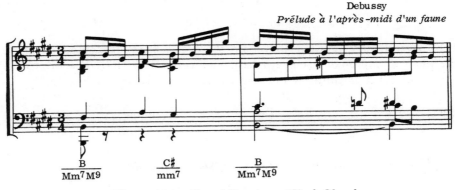

Figure 11.6. *Use of Dominant Ninth Chord*

Figure 11.7, an excerpt from the Grieg *Sailor's Song* (Op. 68, No. 1), has a dominant eleventh chord on the root G, as well as a number of seventh chords.

Figure 11.7. *Use of Dominant Eleventh Chord*

In his song *The Swan*, Grieg employed an eleventh chord followed by a thirteenth; both have the dominant tone as their roots. This excerpt is shown in Figure 11.8. It is interesting to note that Grieg has merely moved the melodic pattern up to a higher pitch while he maintains the same basic chord root.

Figure 11.8. *Use of Dominant Eleventh and Dominant Thirteenth Chords*

ESSENTIAL VOCABULARY

1. tetrad
2. seventh chord
3. seventh
4. leading tone
5. subtonic
6. major-minor seventh chord
7. dominant seventh chord
8. secondary seventh chord
9. third inversion
10. position of the seventh
11. ninth chord
12. eleventh chord
13. thirteenth chord

ASSIGNMENTS

1. Explain the difference in the words *seventh*, *leading tone*, and *subtonic*.

2. Write root position seventh chords with the root and quality shown, **one chord to a measure in the clef indicated.** Use no key signatures, but write **in any necessary accidentals.** Give a root/quality analysis below each chord; make a clear distinction in writing "M" and "m."

A. *Treble Clef*
1) A: mm⁷
2) D: Mm⁷
3) A♭: dd⁷
4) D♭: Mm⁷
5) F: mm⁷
6) B♭: dd⁷
7) D♯: dm⁷
8) E♭: Am⁷
9) G♭: mm⁷
10) C: mm⁷
11) G: dm⁷
12) E: dd⁷
13) C♯: Mm⁷
14) B: mm⁷
15) A♯: Mm⁷

B. *Bass Clef*
1) G♯: mm⁷
2) E♭: dd⁷
3) D♭: Mm⁷
4) F: mm⁷
5) D♯: dm⁷
6) C♯: Mm⁷
7) A♭: Mm⁷
8) B: dd⁷
9) C: Am⁷
10) A: dm⁷
11) F♯: mm⁷
12) B♭: mm⁷
13) G♭: Mm⁷
14) A♯: dd⁷
15) D: mm⁷

C. *Alto Clef*
1) D♯: Mm⁷
2) E♭: mm⁷
3) F: Mm⁷
4) A: dm⁷
5) D: dd⁷
6) G♯: Mm⁷
7) C: dd⁷
8) B♭: dm⁷
9) C♯: mm⁷
10) F♯: mm⁷

D. *Tenor Clef*
1) B: dm⁷
2) E♭: dm⁷
3) F: Mm⁷
4) C♯: dd⁷
5) A♭: Mm⁷
6) D: mm⁷
7) A♯: dd⁷
8) G: mm⁷
9) E: mm⁷
10) B♭: Mm⁷

3. Write the following seventh chords in the arrangements shown and in the clefs indicated:

A. *Treble Clef*

	ROOT	QUALITY	INVERSION	SOPRANO POS.
1)	C	Mm^7	first	fifth
2)	F♯	dd^7	third	octave
3)	C	Mm^7	root pos.	third
4)	B♭	Mm^7	third	third
5)	A♯	mm^7	first	octave
6)	E♭	dd^7	root pos.	third
7)	G♭	mm^7	first	fifth
8)	C♯	Mm^7	root pos.	seventh
9)	D	mm^7	root pos.	third
10)	G	dd^7	second	octave
11)	G♯	Mm^7	first	seventh
12)	A♭	mm^7	third	fifth
13)	D♯	mm^7	second	third
14)	A	Am^7	root pos.	fifth
15)	F	Mm^7	first	seventh

B. *Bass Clef*

	ROOT	QUALITY	INVERSION	SOPRANO POS.
1)	B	dd^7	first	fifth
2)	D♯	dm^7	root pos.	third
3)	G♭	Mm^7	first	fifth
4)	A♭	dd^7	root pos.	seventh
5)	D♭	Mm^7	second	octave
6)	G♯	mm^7	third	third
7)	F♯	Mm^7	third	fifth
8)	E♭	mm^7	root pos.	third
9)	C	Mm^7	third	octave
10)	A♯	Mm^7	first	seventh
11)	B♭	dd^7	second	third
12)	A	Am^7	root pos.	fifth
13)	C♯	mm^7	first	seventh
14)	F	Mm^7	first	octave
15)	G	mm^7	root pos.	third

C. *Alto Clef*

	ROOT	QUALITY	INVERSION	SOPRANO POS.
1)	B♭	dm^7	root pos.	fifth
2)	E♭	Mm^7	third	octave
3)	F♯	dd^7	second	third
4)	A♭	mm^7	root pos.	seventh
5)	D♯	Mm^7	first	octave
6)	G	dm^7	second	seventh
7)	C♯	mm^7	root pos.	third
8)	B	Mm^7	first	fifth
9)	E	dd^7	third	third
10)	D	dd^7	first	octave

D. *Tenor Clef*

	ROOT	QUALITY	INVERSION	SOPRANO POS.
1)	C♭	dm^7	root pos.	third
2)	A♭	Mm^7	first	octave
3)	E	mm^7	root pos.	fifth
4)	G	Mm^7	root pos.	seventh
5)	D	dd^7	second	third

CHORDS OF MORE THAN THREE TONES

Figure 11.9

4. Make a root/quality analysis of each excerpt in Figure 11.9. Disregard chords or single notes that are in parentheses or in boxes; do not include them in your analysis.

[1] From *Twice 55 Community Songs for Male Voices* (Boston: C. C. Birchard and Co.), Copyright © Summy-Birchard Publishing Co. Used by permission.

5. Make a functional analysis of each of the excerpts in Figure 11.10.

(a)

(b)

(c)

(d)

Figure 11.10

12

Establishing

a Key

IN THIS CHAPTER we shall explore some of the factors that establish or determine the key of a piece of music. The concept of key, which includes both tonality and mode, was discussed in some detail in Chapters 6 and 9. You will remember that *tonality* in music is the quality of having one particular tone that is more important than others and is basic to the composition. *Mode* is the aural quality of the tonality, such as major or minor.

PROGRESSION OF CHORDS

The most important factor in the determination of key is the progression of chords, one to another; but the sense of key is reinforced by other factors—the particular set of tones chosen for both the principal melody and the accompaniment, the tones and chords used at the ends of sections throughout the piece, and especially the final tone or chord at the end of the music.

The way that chords progress throughout a piece of music is the basic factor in determining a key. Chords in a key tend to move in the definite pattern discussed in Chapters 8 and 10, a pattern in which tonic, first, and second level chords predominate. A progression that does not fit this flexible pattern does not adequately establish a tonality. The chord progression within each section of the music will strongly imply a certain key, because the progression will seem logical in one key but illogical in any other. In Figure 12.1, the functional analysis in C major shows a logical progression (one that fits the normal pattern of chord movement), with most of the chords as tonic, first, and second level chords. If, on the other hand, the same progression were analyzed in A minor, there would be only one tonic, and not any first level chords; there would, however, be a number of chords in the rarely used fourth and fifth levels. The key of A minor would, therefore, not provide as satisfactory an analysis of this passage as does C major. Analyses in the keys of F major and D minor have been included to show that the progression would be illogical in both of these keys; moreover, there is one chord that does not occur as a diatonic chord in either of these keys.

C Major:	I	IV	I	II	VI	II^7	V	I
A Minor:	III	VI	III	IV	I	IV^7	VII	III
F Major:	V	I	V	VI	III	VI^7	?	V
D Minor:	VII	III	VII	I	V	I^7	?	VII

Figure 12.1. Logical and Illogical Chord Progressions

A certain key is well established if the chords fit the progression pattern known to be typical of it. If the chords do not fit that pattern, the passage may establish another key, or it may leave the sense of the key vague or indeterminate (as in the music of Debussy).

CHOICE OF SCALE TONES

A second factor in establishing and recognizing a key is the selection of tones which are used in the melodic lines of the music. Melodies in diatonic music are built of tones that occur in one key, but not in others. If the tones of a melody coincide with the scale tones of a particular key, the melody will strongly imply that key. Although the accidentals in the key signature must not be neglected, the signature is not really as good an indication of key as the actual tones of the melody. Many times a composer departs from the written signature and establishes an entirely new key by the use of accidentals placed throughout the melodic line. Figure 12.2 shows one line of a Brahms song, in which the key signature is that of C minor; this segment is actually in B minor, however, due to the presence of accidentals.

The alterations from the key signature which regularly occur in minor keys are extremely helpful in identifying a particular key. Only one key, for instance,

Figure 12.2. Melody Tones Showing Different Key from Key Signature

can logically contain both the A sharp and the G natural that occur in Figure 12.3. That key is B minor, in which A sharp is the leading tone and G natural is the un-altered submediant.

Figure 12.3. Key Determination from Alternate Tones in the Minor Scale (Haydn: Symphony No. 104)

The establishment of a key is also affected by the way that short sections of a piece, called *musical phrases*,[1] are brought to a conclusion. A musical phrase is a short, but complete statement of a musical idea, comparable to a sentence in English. Its ending or conclusion is called a *cadence*. Each cadence consists of a pattern of two chords that creates the impression of finality. In establishing a key, the final cadence in a piece of music is more important than earlier cadences, because the root of the last chord is an extremely strong indication of the tonality.

Before considering the different cadence types, let us recount the different factors that affect the establishment of a key. These are 1) the progression of chords throughout the music, 2) the choice of tones that are used in the melody and accompaniment, 3) the cadence patterns that conclude different musical phrases, and 4) the final cadence at the end of the piece of music.

TYPES OF CADENCES

Five types of cadences are commonly used to end phrases of music written in traditional harmonic style. These may be identified by the two chords that comprise the cadence. Each type has minor variations which occur from time to time. A different but similar chord may sometimes be substituted for one of the chords usually found; various substitution possibilities are discussed following the basic definition of each type. If the last chord of the cadence falls on a strong beat of the measure, the cadence is said to be *masculine;* it is *feminine* if the last chord falls on a weak beat.

1. *An authentic cadence* is the progression from a major dominant chord to the tonic at the end of a musical phrase.

$$\text{Major:} \quad V \longrightarrow I$$
$$\text{Minor:} \quad V \longrightarrow I$$
$$\substack{\# \\ 7}$$

It is possible to substitute a few other special chords for the dominant triad with-out disturbing the basic progression of the authentic cadence. The dominant triad, for instance, may be replaced by a tetrad, pentad, or even a more complex chord on the dominant root. Other chords frequently substituted for the dominant include the first inversion of the leading tone triad and the first inversion of the mediant triad.[2]

---

[1] See Chapter 14.
[2] The use of these chords is more fully explained in Chapter 22.

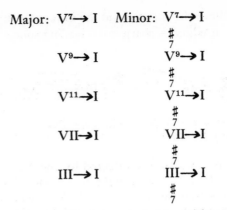

If both the dominant and tonic chords are in root position and the last chord is in the position of the octave, the cadence is a *perfect* authentic cadence. If the last chord is not in the position of the octave, or if either chord is inverted, or if any of the substitutes for the dominant are used, the cadence is *imperfect*. Both perfect and imperfect authentic cadences are shown in Figure 12.4.

2. A *half cadence* is the incomplete close of a phrase which ends on one of the principal triads of the key. Ordinarily the half cadence consists of the progression from the tonic to the major dominant, but the dominant may also be approached from other chords such as IV or II.

Figure 12.4. *Perfect and Imperfect Authentic Cadences*

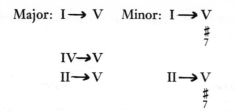

In those rare cases where the final chord of a half cadence is the subdominant rather than the dominant, it is helpful to use the full description: *half cadence on the subdominant*. Figure 12.5 shows two examples of the half cadence, one ending on the dominant, the other on the subdominant.

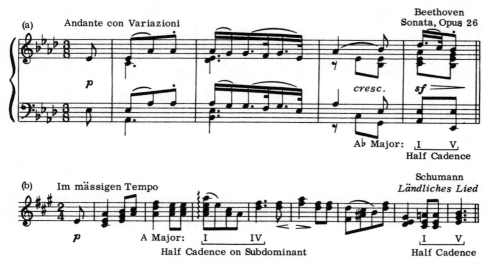

Figure 12.5. *Two Forms of the Half Cadence*

3. A *Phrygian cadence* is the progression in a minor key from the subdominant to the major dominant at the end of a musical phrase.

$$\text{Minor } only: \quad \text{IV} \rightarrow \text{V}$$

In older music, the subdominant triad was normally used in first inversion, but later it was used in root position as well, as is the case in Figure 12.6.

Figure 12.6. *Phrygian Cadence*

4. A *plagal cadence* is the progression from a subdominant chord to the tonic at the end of a musical phrase.

Major
 or :   IV→I
Minor

The *Amen* at the end of a hymn is a plagal cadence. The usual form of the plagal cadence is shown in Figure 12.7. The subdominant chord in this cadence is sometimes replaced by a supertonic seventh chord.

Figure 12.7. *Plagal Cadence*

5. A *deceptive cadence* is the progression from a major dominant chord to the submediant at the end of a musical phrase.

Major: V→VI
Minor: V→VI
         #
         7

Substitutions of other chords in the deceptive cadence are not often seen, but the leading tone or inverted mediant chords may replace the dominant, while the place of the submediant may be taken by a subdominant in the first inversion. The usual form of the deceptive cadence is shown in Figure 12.8.

Figure 12.8. *Usual Form of the Deceptive Cadence*

Another kind of deceptive cadence occurs when the last chord of the cadence pattern is dissonant and must be followed by other chords to achieve resolution, as in the first phrase of Figure 12.9.

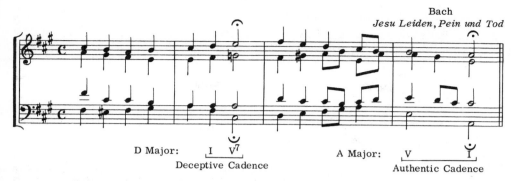

Figure 12.9. Deceptive Cadence Ending on a Dissonant Chord

ESSENTIAL VOCABULARY

1. tonality
2. mode
3. key
4. musical phrase
5. cadence
6. masculine cadence
7. feminine cadence
8. authentic cadence
9. perfect authentic cadence
10. imperfect authentic cadence
11. half cadence
12. half cadence on the subdominant
13. Phrygian cadence
14. plagal cadence
15. deceptive cadence

ASSIGNMENTS

1. Determine the key of each of the following excerpts in Figure 12.10. List the reasons for your choice of key in each case.

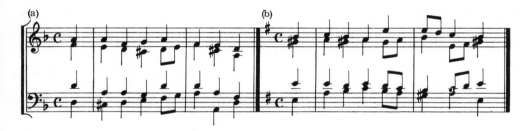

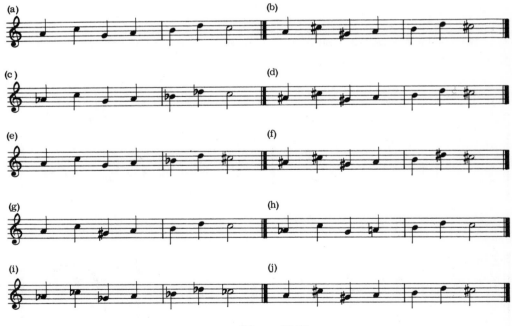

Figure 12.10

2. Name the cadence for each of the excerpts in Figure 12.10.

3. The theoretical melodies in Figure 12.11 have the same notes except for accidentals. State the key in which it would be possible for each example to occur. Assume that only diatonic tones are used, including the altered diatonic tones in minor keys.

Figure 12.11

4. Name the key or keys in which the following chord progressions could occur. Give a functional analysis in each key that you name.

a) E/M, F/M
b) D/M, F♯/m, G/M
c) G♯/d, C♯/M, F♯/m
d) G/m, C/M, F♯/d, G/m
e) E/M, F♯/M, G♯/m
f) E/m, B/M, E/M
g) D/m, A/m, B♭/M, A/M, D/m

5. State the key established by the phrases in Figure 12.12, having the chord progressions shown. Name the cadence in each case; also give a functional analysis of each phrase.

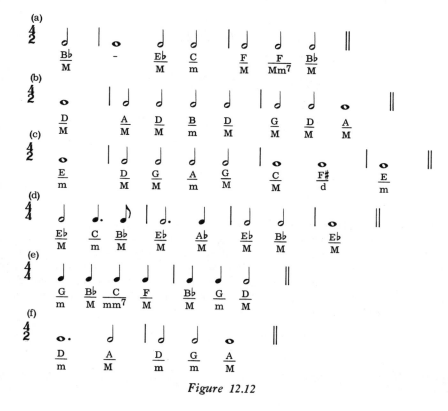

Figure 12.12

13

Principal
Non-Harmonic Tones

Aₗₜₕₒᵤgₕ THE HARMONY of a piece is determined by the tones of the chords used, the structure of each of the different melodic parts often requires the use of tones that are not members of the prevailing chords. These tones are called *non-harmonic tones*. They derive their importance not from their relation to the harmony, but from the melodic lines in which they occur. In Figure 13.1, all the tones of the melody except those marked are members of the underlying chords; those marked with an arrow are non-harmonic tones.

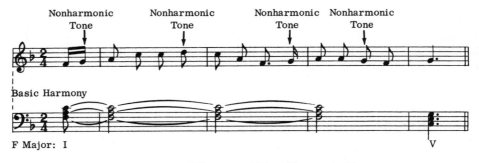

Figure 13.1. The Use of Non-Harmonic Tones

Non-harmonic tones occur between harmonic tones of the melody; the harmonic tones may be members of the same chord or of different chords. The chord tone that precedes a non-harmonic tone is called its *preparation;* the chord tone that follows it is called its *resolution.* Both are shown in Figure 13.2.

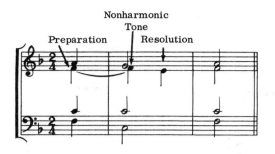

Figure 13.2

For the most part, non-harmonic tones occur singly, lying between two chord tones in the melodic line. Moreover, since non-harmonic tones depend upon the chord tones that precede and follow them, they rarely occur as the first or last note of a musical phrase, nor are they likely to occur before or after a rest. It is also unusual for a non-harmonic tone to be immediately repeated, because by repetition, the tone loses its relationship to its preparation and its resolution. Talented composers have nevertheless used non-harmonic tones successfully in all these unlikely places. It is common for two or more non-harmonic tones to occur at the same time in different voice parts; when they are used in this way, the non-harmonic tones are usually consonant with each other, like those in Figure 13.3.

The two nonharmonic tones in parentheses form the consonant interval of a major third.

Figure 13.3

If a number of non-harmonic tones, such as those in Figure 13.4, make up **an** identifiable chord, the result is sometimes spoken of as a *voice leading chord*,[1] because such a chord is a result of the movement of individual melodic lines rather than a change in the basic harmony.

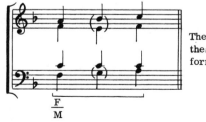

The three nonharmonic tones in parentheses, with the chord tone in the tenor, form a voice leading chord.

Figure 13.4

---

[1] See Chapter 22 for a full discussion of voice leading chords.

PASSING TONES

A *passing tone* (abbreviated P.T.) is a non-harmonic tone that is approached by step and left by step in the same direction. There are two passing tones in Figure 13.5.

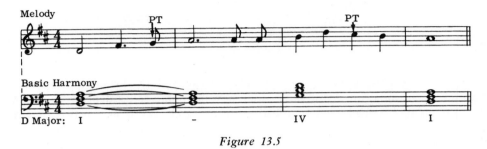

Figure 13.5

The passing tone usually fills in the melodic interval of a third between chord tones with stepwise motion, as shown in Figure 13.6a. Occasionally the interval of a fourth between chord tones will be filled in, as in Figure 13.6b, by two passing tones in succession; these are called *consecutive passing tones*. A passing tone that fills the interval of a major second, as in Figure 13.6c, is a *chromatic passing tone*. When two passing tones occur at the same time, like those in Figure 13.6d, they are called *double passing tones*.

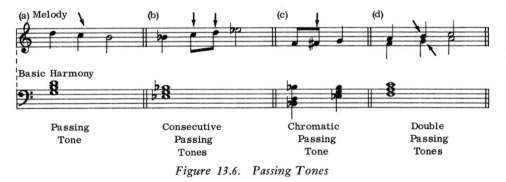

Figure 13.6.   Passing Tones

Passing tones may occur in any voice part. Although they are used most often in a position that is rhythmically weak, *e.g.*, on the last half of a beat, or on a weak beat of the measure, they may also be rhythmically strong, especially when moving downward.[2]

The use of double passing tones, which occur at the same time in two different voices, is quite common; the voices usually move in thirds or sixths.

---

[2] Unfortunately, the terminology for non-harmonic tones is far from standardized. Some authorities, most importantly Walter Piston, do not consider accented non-harmonic tones to be passing tones or neighboring tones, but prefer to call them *appoggiaturas*, provided only that they resolve stepwise. A strong case can be made for either point of view. The definitions used here are the most common ones employed in the United States, according to George Thaddeus Jones in his *Symbols Used in Musical Analysis* (Washington, D.C.: The Catholic University of America, 1964), p. 319.

NEIGHBORING TONES

A *neighboring tone* (N.T.) is a non-harmonic tone that is approached by step in one direction and left by step in the opposite direction, as shown in Figure 13.7.

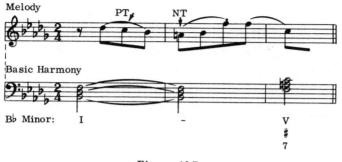

Figure 13.7

A neighboring tone is described as *upper* if it is above the adjacent chord tones, and *lower* if it is below them. The resolution of the neighboring tone has the same letter name as its preparation, although the resolution may be chromatically altered. Neighboring tones are for the most part rhythmically weak. They may occur in any voice part; if two or more neighboring tones occur at the same time, they are called *double* or *triple neighboring tones*. One or more neighboring tones may occur at the same time as passing tones, sometimes forming a voice leading chord. Neighboring tones are also called *auxiliary tones*. Figure 13.8 shows three types of neighboring tones. Lower neighboring tones are more frequent than upper ones. Some musical ornaments, such as trills, mordents, and turns, result from the addition of neighboring tones to a melody.

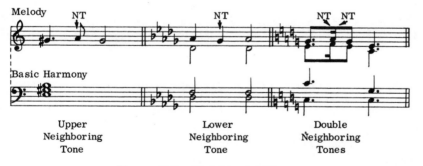

Figure 13.8. Neighboring Tones

SUSPENSIONS

A *suspension* (susp.) is a non-harmonic tone that is approached by holding or by repetition and is left by step, as in the alto part of Figure 13.9.

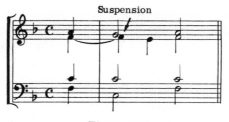

Figure 13.9

Suspensions are named by the intervals the suspension and its resolution form with the bass. The expected resolution of any suspension is always a member of the chord prevailing during the suspension. Common suspensions in upper voices, shown in Figure 13.10, are the 7–6 suspension, the 4–3 suspension, the 9–8 suspension, and more rarely the 2–1 suspension. It is customary to make a distinction between the 9–8 and the 2–1 suspension, although the distinction between simple and compound intervals is otherwise disregarded.

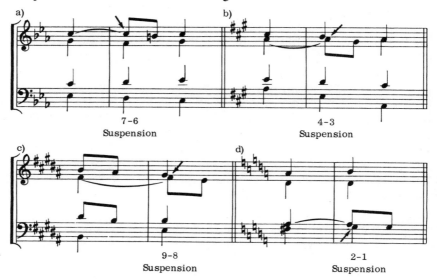

Figure 13.10. Suspensions in Upper Voices

If the suspended note is not in an upper voice, but is in the bass or lowest voice, as in Figure 13.11, it forms the interval of a second with one of the upper voices; this interval becomes a third as the bass moves downward to its resolution. The suspension in the bass is therefore called a 2–3 suspension.

Figure 13.11. Suspension in the Bass

In older music the suspension was controlled by very strict rules. The preparation of the suspension had to be as long or longer than the suspended note itself; the suspension was always resolved by a downward step, never upwards; the suspension always formed a dissonant interval, *i.e.*, a seventh, a fourth, a second, or a ninth with the bass. The suspended note is rhythmically strong, with the preparation and the resolution being in a less accented position.

Later usage of the suspension has been less strict. Upward resolution is not uncommon, and a suspension that resolves in this way can be called a *retardation*. A tone that is not a member of the prevailing chord, if properly approached and left, is now considered a suspension, even if it forms a consonant interval with the bass. The pattern in Figure 13.12 is now considered a suspension, whereas it was once considered a B minor chord in first inversion.

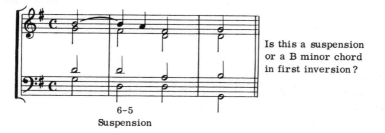

Is this a suspension or a B minor chord in first inversion?

6-5
Suspension

Figure 13.12. *Suspended Note That Is Consonant with the Bass*

The nomenclature of the various suspensions assumes that the other tone of the dissonant interval is retained while the suspension moves to its resolution. If the other tone also moves at the time the suspension resolves, as in Figure 13.13, the situation is called a *suspension with change of bass*. When this occurs, the suspension is no longer called by the same name; the second number in the name is dropped, so that a 7–6 suspension becomes merely a 7– suspension when the bass is changed.

The seventh of a seventh chord is sometimes mistaken for a suspension, for it looks deceptively like a suspension with a change of bass. Remember, however, that a suspension must be able to resolve by step to some member of the *same* chord in which it occurs. A chord seventh, on the other hand, resolves by step to some member of the *next* chord.

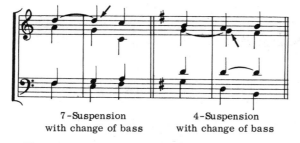

7-Suspension
with change of bass

4-Suspension
with change of bass

Figure 13.13. *Suspension with Change of Bass*

Suspensions that occur in close succession in the same voice, like those in Figure 13.14, are known as *chain suspensions*. The resolution of one suspension becomes the preparation for the next, and so on.

PRINCIPAL NON-HARMONIC TONES   *129*

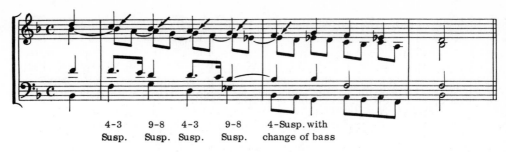

4–3	9–8	4–3	9–8	4–Susp. with
Susp.	Susp.	Susp.	Susp.	change of bass

Figure 13.14. Chain Suspensions

SUSPENSION ORNAMENTS

A suspension may be ornamented in several ways, as shown in Figure 13.15, before it reaches its actual resolution. The melodic line which has the suspension may move from the suspended tone to another chord tone before moving to the resolution tone. Or, it may move to the resolution sooner than would be expected, thus anticipating the resolution tone. The resolution may be adorned further with a lower neighboring tone. The suspension resolution may also be preceded by a note that moves by step to the resolution tone.

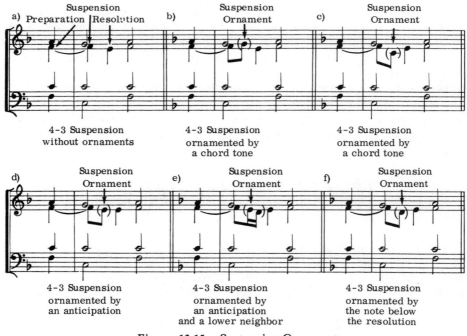

Figure 13.15. Suspension Ornaments

ANALYSIS PROBLEMS WITH NON-HARMONIC TONES

There are many instances in music where doubt arises in the analysis of non-harmonic tones. Is there a non-harmonic tone, or has the chord itself changed? Many chords, especially tetrads and pentads, began as triads with non-harmonic tones, but later came to be recognized as chord patterns. One of these ambiguous situations involves the seventh of a chord that is introduced as a passing tone.

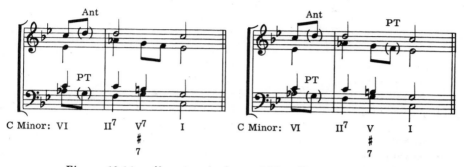

Figure 13.16. Alternate Analyses of Non-Harmonic Tones

Is the F in the alto of Figure 13.16 a non-harmonic tone, or does the chord change to a dominant seventh chord on the second half of the second beat? Since no clear choice is obvious, a method of analysis should be adopted and used as consistently as possible. The chord may be considered a tetrad, being analyzed as V^7; or as an alternative, tones added after the rest of the chord is sounded may be treated as non-harmonic tones, resulting in the analysis of V.

Another ambiguous situation occurs when the change of only one or two tones causes an apparent change of chord, as in Figure 13.17.

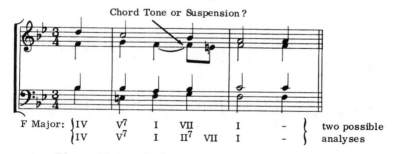

Figure 13.17. Analysis of an Ambiguous Situation

In the alto of Figure 13.17, the tied eighth note could be either a 7–6 suspension in the leading tone triad, or the seventh of a supertonic seventh chord. (The fifth of the II^7 chord is often omitted.) Again, no clear choice is evident. The speed of the music is an important factor in such a situation. If the music is slow, the tones in question appear to have more importance as chord tones; if it is faster, the same tones seem more like non-harmonic material. Another thing to consider is whether the chord progression is a logical one if the tone in question is analyzed as part of the chord.

Where there is ambiguity in analysis because of the presence of non-harmonic tones, the analyst should adopt a consistent procedure, chosen from the two or three possible alternatives. It must be recognized that in such situations, each analysis may have its virtues. The choice of one analysis should not make one disregard the advantages of a different analysis of the musical structure.

ESSENTIAL VOCABULARY

1. non-harmonic tones
2. preparation
3. resolution
4. passing chord
5. principal non-harmonic tones
6. passing tone
7. double passing tones
8. consecutive passing tones
9. neighboring tone
10. auxiliary tone
11. suspension
12. 7–6 suspension
13. 4–3 suspension
14. 9–8 suspension
15. 2–1 suspension
16. 2–3 suspension
17. retardation
18. suspension with change of bass
19. chain suspensions
20. suspension ornament

ASSIGNMENTS

1. Make a functional analysis of each of the excerpts in Figure 13.18. Enclose each non-harmonic tone in parentheses and label it.

Figure 13.18

2. Make a root/quality analysis of the excerpts in Figure 13.19. (Do not attempt a functional analysis, as that would require knowledge of material not yet studied.) Enclose all non-harmonic tones in parentheses and label them.

Figure 13.19

14

Basic Units of
Musical Form

BECAUSE A PIECE of music exists in time rather than in space, its sounds move irrevocably into the past as we listen. The music becomes intelligible only in the memory of what has been heard and in the expectation of what is to be heard. *Musical form*, or the plan of the music, becomes evident to the listener as he hears a musical idea reused and contrasted with other musical ideas, as he realizes that what he is hearing at the moment is either the same as, or different from, what he has already heard.

Patterns of musical form have changed from time to time, just as other aspects of music have changed. Early music depended upon the poetical structure of the text that was to be sung; religious music was often shaped to the practical demands of the liturgy; and dance music developed regular, symmetrical forms that were influenced by the steps and movements of the dancers. Art music has drawn from all these sources to develop formal patterns of its own, such as the theme and variations, the rondo, the minuet and trio form, and the sonata-allegro form. Each of these forms or plans of art music is dependent on smaller structural units, and it is these smaller units that concern us now.

THE PHRASE

The briefest complete unit of thought in writing English is the sentence; in music it is the musical *phrase*. A phrase may be recognized by two characteristics: its essential unity and its definite conclusion in a cadence. Most phrases end in one of the typical cadences described in Chapter 12. Musical phrases can be of varying lengths, but the music of the eighteenth and nineteenth centuries usually has phrases that are four measures long. If the tempo is very slow, two-measure phrases are possible, as are eight-measure phrases in fast tempo. Phrases that do not fit these regular patterns are less common.

COMPONENTS OF THE PHRASE: FIGURE AND MOTIVE

Within a musical phrase, there are smaller units of form which lack the completeness that marks the phrase itself; these smaller units lack a cadence or conclusion. One such unit is the *figure*, a brief but recognizable musical entity which may contain several notes or perhaps only two. A figure is recognized, not by its specific length, but by the fact that it constitutes a single, separate, identifiable musical idea.

If a musical figure is used in such a way that it is basic to the structure of the phrase or of the piece of music as a whole, it is called a *motive*. The figure and the motive do not differ in their length or in their nature, but in their use; a figure becomes a motive if it is reused in a way that makes it significant to the over-all structure of the music. There are numerous ways in which a figure may be employed so that it becomes a motive. It may, for instance, merely be repeated; it may be used at a different pitch, or it may be modified in some way. Figure 14.1 shows several phrases that are constructed of motives.

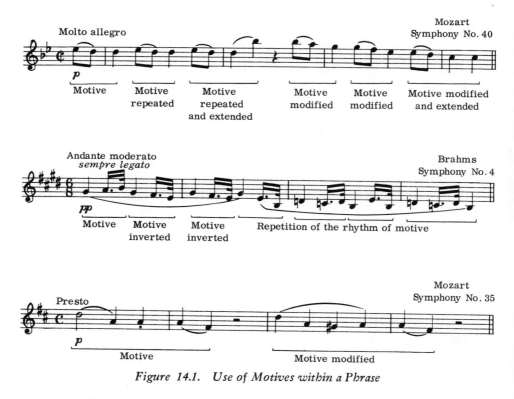

Figure 14.1. Use of Motives within a Phrase

Some musical phrases consist of two distinct segments. The terms *semi-phrase* and *phrase member* are sometimes used to identify these segments. Each of the phrases in Figure 14.1 is divided into two semi-phrases.

FORMS LONGER THAN THE PHRASE

Because a single musical phrase is too short for adequate musical expression, composers combine several phrases to construct larger musical units—the *period,* the *double period,* and the *phrase group.*

A *period* consists of two musical phrases related by the use of similar musical ideas. The first phrase has an inconclusive cadence, such as a half cadence or a deceptive cadence; but the second phrase comes to a more definite close, usually an authentic cadence. The first of the two phrases is called the *antecedent phrase;* the second is called the *consequent phrase.* In some period forms the two phrases begin in similar fashion, giving rise to the term *parallel construction,* shown in Figure 14.2.

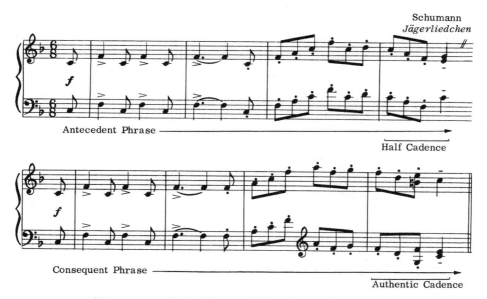

Figure 14.2.   Period Form with Parallel Construction

In other cases the two phrases, although obviously related, correspond to *statement* and *response.* Figure 14.3 shows this kind of period construction.

Consequent Phrase

Authentic Cadence

Figure 14.3.   Period Form with Statement-Response Construction

The *double period* is a symmetrical form consisting of two related periods. Here again, the final cadence is definite, with the interior cadences being less conclusive. In large works such as symphonies or sonatas, the principal idea or theme is often cast in double period form. Figure 14.4 shows the first part of a Beethoven piano sonata, a section in double period form. Notice that each of the periods shows statement and response, but that the two periods are quite similar. The first period ends in a half cadence (I→V), but the second has the expected authentic cadence.

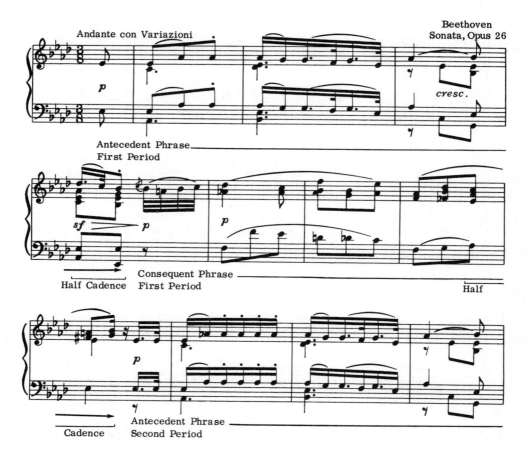

Consequent Phrase ——————————————————

Half Cadence   Second Period   Authentic Cadence

Figure 14.4 Double Period Form

A *phrase group* is made up of three independent phrases which have enough similarity to form a coherent unit. Less frequent than either the period or double period forms, the phrase group lacks their symmetry, so it must depend to a greater extent on musical content for its essential unity. The pattern of cadences is important to its construction, with only the final cadence being conclusive.

EXTENSION OF BASIC FORMS

Each of the basic units of musical form, *i.e.*, the phrase, the period, etc., may be slightly enlarged by the process known as *extension*. An extension consists of musical material borrowed from whatever is being extended. New or extraneous material does not properly extend any of these basic forms. The extension of a phrase is often a mere repetition of the cadence pattern. If the extension precedes the phrase, then it must anticipate what is to follow. The period and double period forms are normally extended by repeating, perhaps in modified form, one or more of the phrases that constitute them. Figure 14.5 shows Beethoven's use of an extension. The phrase is eight measures long, extended twice by repetition of the cadence pattern.

Beethoven
Opus 2, No. 1, measures 9–20

Figure 14.5. Phrase Extension

The basic structural units of phrase, period, and double period are not extensive enough to constitute a piece of music longer than a simple hymn or folk song. Larger pieces are built by combining the basic units into longer sections, which are in turn combined to make the piece as a whole. The plan or arrangement of the sections is the *form* of the piece. The number of forms known to have been used at different times in the history of music is quite large, but many of them have become obsolete, and are only rarely used in music heard today. The more common plans of construction can be divided into *small forms* and *large forms*.

SMALL FORMS

Small forms, sometimes called *song forms*, consist of sections that are phrases, periods, and double periods. There are two basic plans, which are subject to considerable alteration. The simplest is *binary form*, also called *dance form* and *two-part song form*. It has two musical statements that differ in actual content, but are alike in mood and style. The essence of the form is a statement and a related response. Either the statement or the response, or both of them, may be repeated without disturbing the basic plan.

The other basic plan is *ternary form*, also called *aria form* or *three-part song form;* it consists of two contrasting musical statements. One idea is stated at the beginning, to be stated again after a contrasting section has been heard. The plan is often represented by the letters ABA. Because of the symmetical nature of the plan, the two sections may be quite different in character.

Both binary and ternary forms may be expanded slightly by supplementary material such as introductions and conclusions, or by transitions from one idea to another. As long as these remain subordinate to the main statements, the basic form is not disturbed.

LARGE FORMS

Large forms include the *rondo*, the *theme and variations*, and the *sonata-allegro form*. Large forms differ from small forms principally in the complexity of their component sections. A large form may have a first section that is a small ternary form in itself. Moreover, the amount of extra material, such as transitions, introductions, and conclusions, is generally much greater in large forms than in small ones.

A *rondo* consists of the alternation of a recurrent musical statement, called the *rondo theme*, with one or two contrasting ideas. Different kinds of rondos are depicted in letters such as ABA, ABACA, and ABACABA; in each case, the recurrent idea is represented by the letter A. The simplest of the rondo forms (ABA) differs from simple ternary form by greater complexity and scope. Most rondos have a main statement that is easily recognized when it returns. Sometimes the recurrent theme is varied slightly each time it occurs. Examples of rondo form may be found in the third movements of all four Brahms symphonies, and in the last movements of concertos such as the Beethoven Violin Concerto.

The *theme and variations* form is simple in concept, but difficult in construction. A simple idea, often of period or double period length, is stated, then restated differently, over and over, until its possibilities for musical expression have been exhausted by the composer. The theme and variation form occurs in the second movement of Haydn's "Surprise" Symphony, Beethoven's Fifth Symphony, and his Seventh Symphony. There are also uses of this form in the *Diabelli Variations* by Beethoven, the *Goldberg Variations* by Bach, and the *Variations on a Theme by Haydn* by Brahms.

The most common of the large forms is *sonata-allegro form*, so named because it occurs frequently in the allegro movements of sonatas and symphonies. Sonata-allegro form consists of three sections—*exposition, development*, and *recapitulation*. The exposition presents two musical ideas, usually of a contrasting nature. The development employs the musical content of the exposition, but presents it in various guises and in different keys. The recapitulation reaffirms the original statement. An important factor in sonata-allegro form is the contrast between the principal key and the key of the dominant. The second theme is presented in the dominant key in the exposition,[1] but is stated in the tonic in the recapitulation. In its classic form as used by Haydn, Mozart, and Beethoven, the exposition is repeated so that the two themes are thoroughly familiar before their development begins. Beethoven used the sonata-allegro plan for the first movements of all nine of his symphonies; it is frequently used in other movements as well. The form also occurs in sonatas and string quartets by Haydn, Mozart, Beethoven, Schubert, and many other composers.

ESSENTIAL VOCABULARY

1. musical form
2. phrase
3. figure
4. motive
5. semi-phrase
6. phrase member
7. period
8. double period
9. phrase group
10. antecedent phrase
11. consequent phrase
12. parallel construction
13. statement and response construction
14. extension
15. small forms
16. large forms
17. song forms

---

[1] If the first theme is in a minor key, the second theme is usually in the relative major instead of the dominant.

18. binary form
19. dance form
20. two-part song form
21. ternary form
22. aria form
23. three-part song form

24. rondo
25. theme and variations
26. sonata-allegro form
27. exposition
28. development
29. recapitulation

ASSIGNMENTS

1. Analyze the formal structure of each of the following musical excerpts:

   a) Schumann: *Album for the Young*
     No. 3, "Ditty"—measures 1-8
     No. 8, "The Wild Horseman"—measures 1-8
     No. 19, "Little Romance"—measures 1-8
     No. 24, "Harvest Song"—measures 1-8
     No. 4, "Choral"—measures 1-16
     No. 6, "Poor Orphan"—measures 1-8

   b) Mozart: Piano Sonatas
     No. 5 (K.189h), First Movement—measures 1-8
     No. 7 (K.315c), Last Movement—measures 1-16
     No. 9 (K.205b), Last Movement—measures 1-8
     No. 13 (K.547a), First Movement—measures 1-16
     No. 15 (K.576), First Movement—measures 1-16
     No. 16 (K.300i), First Movement—measures 1-16

   c) Beethoven: Piano Sonatas
     Op. 13, Last Movement—measures 1-8
     Op. 31, No. 3, Second Movement—measures 1-8

   d) Mendelssohn: *Songs Without Words*
     Op. 30, No. 3—measures 4-10
     Op. 38, No. 2—measures 1-8

15

Modulation

Much has been said in previous chapters about the importance of tonality as a unifying factor in a piece of music. Chapter 12 was devoted to the ways in which tonality is established by the composer and recognized by the listener. Only very brief pieces of music, however, can remain in a single key without becoming monotonous. The construction of larger musical works requires not one but several tonalities, arranged in an artful pattern. In most cases the music establishes a tonality, departs from it, and then returns. In long pieces, several changes of key are the normal pattern. Such changes of tonality are called *modulations*. A mere change of mode, such as from F major to F minor, is not a modulation. Modulation must involve a change in the keynote or tonal center of the music.

In traditional harmony, most modulations are to keys that have many tones in common with the previously established key. Such keys are said to be *closely related*. Specifically, the group of keys considered to be closely related includes the tonic, the dominant, and the subdominant and their relative major or relative minor keys. This group of six keys includes all the keys whose key signatures differ by no more than one accidental from that of the home key.

DURATION OF MODULATIONS

Modulations may differ in their duration, and the change may be accomplished by any of several means. We distinguish three durations of modulation. The briefest is called a *transient modulation*. A more conclusive change of tonality, usually somewhat longer, is called a *cadential modulation*. The most extensive is called a *complete modulation*.

A transient modulation moves to a new key and immediately back to the previous key (occasionally to another new key). The new key is 1) not firmly established, nor 2) is the new key employed for any sizeable portion of the music. In a sense, a transient modulation consists merely of borrowing one, two, or even three chords from a closely related key. Many authorities prefer to think of these temporary, fragmentary excursions into other keys as merely an expansion of the harmonic vocabulary of the original key, rather than as a modulation or actual change of tonality. If one remembers that it takes some time to establish a key firmly, this reasoning is quite logical. The transitory nature of this sort of modulation is easily seen in Figure 15.1. The last chord in measure two is not a diatonic chord in the key of A flat major because of the presence of the G flat in the alto. This chord is the clue to a transient modulation to the key of D flat major; it can also be considered as a chord borrowed from the closely related key of D flat.

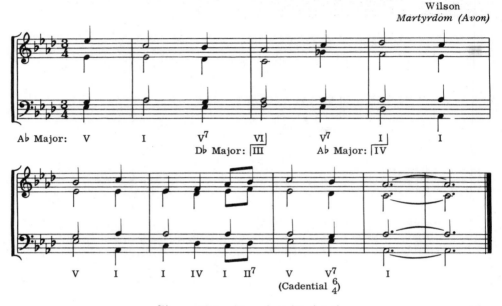

Figure 15.1. Transient Modulation

A cadential modulation 1) firmly establishes a new key by a standard cadence at the end of the musical phrase, but 2) it does not employ the new key beyond the cadence. After the cadence the piece modulates again, usually back to the previous key. Modulations like this are quite common in short pieces such as hymns and folk songs. Figure 15.2 shows Bach's use of a cadential modulation in one of his chorale harmonizations.

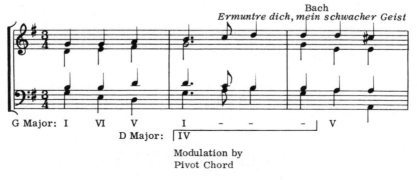

Modulation by
Pivot Chord

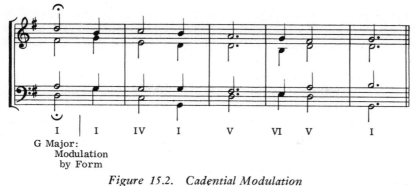

Figure 15.2. Cadential Modulation

A complete modulation 1) establishes a new key, and 2) uses that new key after it has been established. In most cases of complete modulation the new key continues beyond the musical phrase in which the change takes place. A complete modulation may use the new key for only a phrase or so, but more often the new key is employed for a major theme or other large section of a piece. Bach's use of the complete modulation is shown in Figure 15.3.

Figure 15.3. Complete Modulation

METHODS OF MODULATION

Modulation may be brought about in many different ways. Only the three most common methods of modulation will be discussed here—modulation by *pivot chord*, modulation by *form*, and modulation by *chromatic alteration*.

Modulation by pivot chord, the most common of all types, employs a chord that occurs as a normal chord in both the old and the new keys. For a chord to act as a pivot, it must have a different function in each key, but the same root and quality. Only one chord is actually involved, even though it is given two analyses. For example, the VI chord in a major key may become the II chord in the major key on the dominant; or it may become the III chord in the major key on the subdominant. Sometimes several chords in a modulating passage are common to both keys; in such cases the pivot chord is usually, but not always, the chord before the first chord that cannot logically be a part of the old key. The choice of pivot chord depends on the aural recognition of the new key. Figures 15.1 and 15.3 both have modulations that are accomplished by use of pivot chords.

A modulation that occurs after the cadence of a phrase or larger section of music is called *modulation by form*. The phrase preceding the modulation ends with a cadence in one key, but the succeeding phrase begins in another key. Modulation by form is often employed to return to a key which has previously been established, but from which departure has been made. The abruptness of a key change without a pivot chord is softened by the division or break between phrases. Figure 15.2 has a typical modulation by form.

The third method of key change is *chromatic modulation*, which requires a half step chromatic movement in one of the voice parts. The abruptness of the key change in this case is softened by the smooth voice leading of the chromatic half step. Figure 15.4 has a chromatic modulation in the last phrase, caused by the chromatic movement from F to F♯ in the bass voice in the sixth measure. The modulation in the second measure uses a pivot chord.

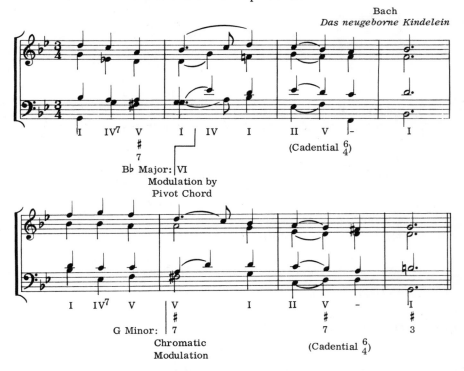

Figure 15.4. Modulation by Chromatic Inflection

ESSENTIAL VOCABULARY

1. modulation
2. closely related keys
3. transient modulation
4. cadential modulation
5. complete modulation
6. pivot chord modulation
7. form modulation
8. chromatic modulation

ASSIGNMENTS

1. Fill in the blanks in the following sentences:

   a) IV in B major becomes III in _____.
      Root/quality is _____.

   b) I in E minor becomes VII in _____.
      $\overset{\sharp}{3}$
      Root/quality is _____.

   c) II in F♯ minor becomes VII in _____.
      $\overset{\sharp}{7}$
      Root/quality is _____.

   d) IV in A minor becomes VI in _____.
      Root/quality is _____.

   e) I in A major becomes VI in _____.
      Root/quality is _____.

   f) V in C♯ minor becomes IV in _____.
      $\overset{\sharp}{7}$ $\overset{\sharp}{6}$
      Root/quality is _____.

   g) V is G major becomes VI in _____.
      Root/quality is _____.

   h) II in B♭ minor becomes VI in _____.
      $\overset{\sharp}{6}$
      Root/quality is _____.

   i) I in G♭ major becomes VI in _____.
      Root/quality is _____.

   j) III in A♭ major becomes VI in _____.
      Root/quality is _____.

   k) VI in B minor becomes IV in _____.
      Root/quality is _____.

   l) III in C minor becomes V in _____.
      Root/quality is _____.

   m) VII in G minor becomes II in _____.
      $\overset{\sharp}{7}$
      Root/quality is _____.

   n) IV in B♭ major becomes III in _____.
      Root/quality is _____.

   o) II in C♯ minor becomes V in _____.
      $\overset{\sharp}{6}$
      Root/quality is _____.

p) VI in F major becomes IV in _____.
Root/quality is _____.

q) V in D minor becomes VI in _____.
$\overset{\sharp}{7}$
Root/quality is _____.

r) VII in F♯ major becomes II in _____.
Root/quality is _____.

s) IV in E major becomes III in _____.
Root/quality is _____.

t) VII in G minor becomes V in _____.
Root/quality is _____.

2. Fill in the blanks in the following sentences:

a) III in E♭ minor becomes _____ in C♭ major.
Root/quality is _____.

b) VI in A major becomes _____ in D major.
Root/quality is _____.

c) IV in B♭ minor becomes _____ in G minor.
$\overset{\sharp}{6}$
Root/quality is _____.

d) VII in C major becomes _____ in A minor.
Root/quality is _____.

e) IV in F major becomes _____ in C minor.
Root/quality is _____.

f) VI in D minor becomes _____ in C major.
$\overset{\sharp}{6}$
Root/quality is _____.

g) V in A minor becomes _____ in C major.
Root/quality is _____.

h) II in C♯ major becomes _____ in A♯ minor.
Root/quality is _____.

i) II in F minor becomes _____ in D minor.
$\overset{\sharp}{6}$
Root/quality is _____.

j) I in D major becomes _____ in F♯ minor.
Root/quality is _____.

k) IV in C minor becomes _____ in D♭ major.
Root/quality is _____.

l) III in B♭ minor becomes _____ in A♭ major.
Root/quality is _____.

m) V in D♭ major becomes _____ in F minor.
Root/quality is _____.

n) III in D♯ minor becomes _____ in B major.
Root/quality is _____.

o) II in A♭ minor becomes _____ in G♭ major.
$\overset{\sharp}{6}$
Root/quality is _____.

p) VI in E♭ major becomes ＿＿＿ in G minor.
 Root/quality is ＿＿＿.

q) II in B minor becomes ＿＿＿ in D major.
 Root/quality is ＿＿＿.

r) IV in E major becomes ＿＿＿ in C♯ minor.
 Root/quality is ＿＿＿.

s) II in F♯ major becomes ＿＿＿ in B major.
 Root/quality is ＿＿＿.

t) VI in G minor becomes ＿＿＿ in B♭ major.
 Root/quality is ＿＿＿.

16

Basic Elements of
Musical Texture

A PIECE OF music is constructed by an artful organization or arrangement of musical ideas. Music primarily expresses non-verbal, non-rational ideas through patterns of sounds. Some of these patterns are melodies, some are chord progressions, some are composed of rhythmic movement. It is the interweaving of these and other purely musical materials that creates the fabric of a piece of music. The finished music is analogous to a tapestry, with its multi-colored threads woven in and out in intricate designs that together comprise the whole. When musical ideas occur one after the other, their arrangement or organization is called *musical form*, discussed in Chapter 14. When the musical ideas occur at the same time, their arrangement creates *musical texture*. A musical idea that constitutes only one portion of the total fabric is a *textural element*. Thus we distinguish a single element of texture from the whole, which is a composite of all the separate elements that occur at the same time. There are many such elements of musical texture, but *melody, countermelody*, and *accompaniment* are the most important ones. In this chapter, we shall discuss only these basic elements, leaving the less common aspects of texture to Chapter 25.

The most important of all elements of musical texture is melody. Stravinsky, in his book *Poetics of Music*, says: "I am beginning to think, in full agreement with the general public, that melody must keep its place at the summit of the hierarchy of elements that make up music. Melody is the most essential of these elements . . ."[1] Most other elements of music serve only to provide the main melody with a proper setting. An accompaniment furnishes both harmony and rhythmic movement as background support of the melody. A countermelody forms an element of contrast that makes the principal melody more perceptible.

---

[1] Igor Stravinsky, *Poetics of Music* (Cambridge, Mass.: Harvard University Press, 1942), p. 43. Used by permission of the President and Fellows of Harvard College, copyright owners.

A melody may be surrounded by a complex musical fabric, by a simple combination of textural elements, or it may occur alone, the only textural element present. Early music often consisted of nothing but melody. The music of the troubadours, trouvères, and Minnesingers was *monophonic* music, that is, it consisted of melody alone. The same was true of the chants of the medieval church. Although we rarely stop to think about it, much of the informal music of our own time is nothing more than melody—a young man singing in the shower, a mother humming her baby to sleep, or a boy whistling to keep up his courage as he walks home on a dark night.

Figure 16.1 shows one of the famous melodies of the medieval church, the sequence[2] for Easter Sunday, which is sung without accompaniment.

Figure 16.1. Melody of Easter Sequence, Victimae paschali laudes[3]

Later composers have also employed melody alone, although they have rarely built entire pieces in this way. One particularly frequent procedure has been the introduction of a melody in isolation, with other elements of the texture added later. Nearly all fugues begin with a solitary statement of the principal melody, or subject, as in Figure 16.2.

Figure 16.2. Melody Alone in a Fugue Subject

Each of the examples in Figure 16.3 shows a piece of music that begins with melody alone. All of these pieces become more complex as they add other textural elements.

---

[2] A setting of a religious text that occurs after the *Alleluia* of the Roman Mass.
[3] From *Plainsong for Schools* (Desclée et Cie., Tournai, Belgium), p. 83. Copyright 1933. Used by permission.

Figure 16.3. Melody Occurring Alone

MELODY AND COUNTERMELODY

Historically, the first enlargement of the musical texture was the addition of a countermelody to the principal melodic idea. Ever since its first introduction in Western music, countermelody has continued to be one of the most important of textural elements. A countermelody may be higher or lower in pitch than the principal one, or the two may be so nearly even in pitch that they seem interwoven. It is possible to have more than one countermelody at the same time; music of the sixteenth century consisted largely of several simultaneous melodies. For the present, however, we shall concern ourselves only with a melody and a single countermelody.

The relation between a melody and its countermelody depends upon the style of the composition. In the Middle Ages, for instance, melody and countermelody were related by having a perfect consonance—octave, fifth, or unison—at the beginning of each rhythmic pattern, the pattern being roughly equivalent to our modern measure. In the Renaissance, consonant and dissonant intervals controlled the two melodies. In the period of harmonic music with which we are concerned, the two melodic lines are controlled by the chords which they imply.

Both melody and countermelody include chord tones and non-harmonic tones. In this harmonic style, chord tones that occur in both melody and countermelody must be drawn from the chord that forms the prevailing harmony. Whatever independence the two melodies have must result from their rhythm, their non-harmonic tones, and the direction of their melodic movement. Figure 16.4 shows a simple melody and countermelody taken from a Bach fugue for organ, while Figure 16.5 is from Beethoven's *"Eroica" Variations*. In both examples, the chords to which both melody and countermelody are related are shown by a root/quality analysis.

Figure 16.4.   *Melody and Countermelody*

Figure 16.5.   *Melody and Countermelody*

Bass Countermelody

A countermelody that occurs in the bass is a particularly important kind of countermelody. In addition to its melodic function, it serves to imply the harmony that underlies the entire musical structure. The bass countermelody has had special significance throughout the history of harmonic music. In the seventeenth and eighteenth centuries, music often had only two written parts, a melody and a bass. Any further accompaniment was improvised at the time of performance on a harmony instrument such as the harpsichord. The bass line in such pieces was called a *thorough-bass* or, in Italian, a *basso continuo*. Sometimes Arabic numerals were written above the bass melody in order to clarify the harmony that the composer intended. When the numbers were present, the bass was said to be *figured*.

Figure 16.6 shows a melody and its bass from Bach's Cantata No. 78, *Jesu, der du meine Seele*. Although the melody and the bass are both related to an implied harmonic progression, the two melodies are quite independent in rhythm and direction.

Figure 16.6. *Melody and Bass Countermelody*

By the nineteenth century, bass figuration was no longer used, but the bass countermelody maintained its importance in the total musical texture. Figure 16.7 shows a melody and its bass from Brahms's Symphony No. 4. The two melodic ideas differ in rhythm and contour, but are related by the chord structure that they imply.

Imitative Countermelody

An *imitative countermelody* is another important type of countermelody. This is the restatement of the principal melody in another voice or register, so that the latter part of the melody forms a countermelody to its own beginning. All rounds and canons employ this device. Many times composers have employed imitative countermelodies in as many as three, four, or more voices, so that the imitative effect builds up in pyramid fashion. Figure 16.8 shows the use of an imitative countermelody.

Figure 16.7. Melody and Bass Countermelody

Figure 16.8. Melody and Imitative Countermelody

BASIC ELEMENTS OF MUSICAL TEXTURE

MELODY AND ACCOMPANIMENT

There is much music that consists of a melody and an accompaniment, a combination of textural elements common not only in popular and folk music but in much serious music as well. The accompaniment has the dual purpose of furnishing both harmonic and rhythmic movement to support the melody. Although it is rare that the two elements, harmony and rhythm, are separated in an accompaniment, it will be helpful if we consider some cases in which the accompaniment supplies only one of these musical components—either harmony or rhythm.

Harmonic Accompaniment

A purely *harmonic accompaniment* supplies no sense of beat or rhythmic movement, even though it may conform to the prevailing meter. It normally states a harmonic progression through sustained chords. The excerpt from Rimsky-Korsakov's *Scheherazade* in Figure 16.9 has a melody in the bassoon. The thin harmony is assigned only to the double-basses. The harmony in this case is simple

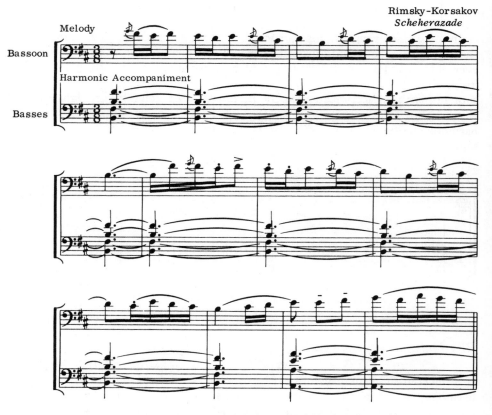

Figure 16.9. Melody and Harmonic Accompaniment[4]

---

[4] Reprinted from the Eulenberg Pocket Score of the complete *Scheherazade* with permission of C. F. Peters Corporation, New York, N.Y. 10016.

and static; the first chord change comes only after ten whole measures. (A short B minor chord on the harp has been omitted from the first measure.)

The second movement of Dvořák's "New World" Symphony, shown in Figure 16.10, has a progression of slow chords that forms a purely harmonic accompaniment. The melody is played on the English horn; the strings have the harmonic accompaniment.

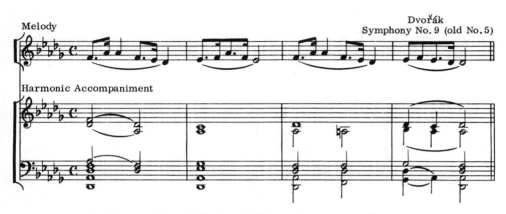

Figure 16.10.   Melody and Harmonic Accompaniment

In some cases, simple hymns for instance, harmonic accompaniment may reflect the rhythm of the melody instead of merely sustaining chords. It does not, however, add anything to the rhythm which is not already present in the melody itself. The hymn tune *Bread of Life*, shown in Figure 16.11, has a melody in the soprano, with an accompaniment in the lower three voices. Although there is a rhythmic pattern in the accompanying voices, the accompaniment is essentially harmonic in function, for the lower voices merely reflect the rhythm of the soprano, adding nothing that is either new or different.

Figure 16.11.   Melody and Harmonic Accompaniment

Rhythmic Accompaniment

If an accompaniment provides only rhythmic interest, without stating pitch or harmony, it is a purely *rhythmic accompaniment*. Such usage is found in the music for a drum and bugle corps, although it is rare in serious music. A few examples do occur, however, and one of them is a cornet solo in Stravinsky's *Petrouchka*, shown in Figure 16.12; the only accompaniment is furnished by the snare drum.

BASIC ELEMENTS OF MUSICAL TEXTURE   *157*

Figure 16.12. Melody and Rhythmic Accompaniment[5]

Combined Harmonic and Rhythmic Accompaniment

In most cases, an accompaniment supplies both harmonic and rhythmic interest to music. This dual function of accompaniment is most easily seen in orchestral music, in which the composer has assigned the rhythmic function of the accompaniment to one group of instruments and the harmonic function to another group. A particularly clear example occurs in Aaron Copland's *El Salón México*, Figure 16.13. Here the melody is played in octaves by violins and cellos. The

Figure 16.13. Melody with Separate Harmonic and Rhythmic Accompaniments[6]

harmonic accompaniment is formed by sustained chords in the woodwinds and horns. Other strings, although playing the same chord, have the primary function of supplying a rhythmic pattern to accompany the melody.

In keyboard music and in much orchestral music, the harmonic and rhythmic functions of the accompaniment are often inseparable. The rhythm of the accompaniment in Figure 16.14 is enunciated through a chord structure, while harmony is stated in a rhythmic pattern.

Figure 16.14. Melody with Combined Harmonic and Rhythmic Accompaniment

Melody, countermelody, and accompaniment (both harmonic and rhythmic) are only a few of the elements of musical texture. These are, however, the basic elements found in almost all music. Other textural elements merely enrich and ornament these basic components.

ESSENTIAL VOCABULARY

1. musical texture
2. textural element
3. melody
4. countermelody
5. accompaniment
6. bass countermelody
7. thorough-bass
8. basso continuo
9. figured bass
10. imitative countermelody
11. harmonic accompaniment
12. rhythmic accompaniment

ASSIGNMENTS

1. Copy out both the melody and the bass of five hymn tunes. In each case, decide whether the bass is a real countermelody or merely part of a harmonic accompaniment. State the reasons for your choice.

2. Explain the effect of the piano's damper pedal on the texture of Figure 16.14.

3. Rewrite Figure 16.14 so that there is a melody and a purely harmonic accompaniment. Keep the same harmony.

4. Rewrite Figure 16.10 so that the accompaniment consists of arpeggios that provide rhythmic movement as well as harmony.

17

Melody Analysis

No MATTER HOW primitive or sophisticated music may be, melody is one of its most important elements. Melodies differ greatly depending upon the geographical source of the music, the time in which the melody was written, the style of the music, and the instrument for which the melody was conceived. Each kind of music has its own melodic idiom, so it is fruitless to say that vocal melody is better or worse than instrumental melody, that Oriental melody is better or worse than Western melody, or that motivic melody is better or worse than folk melody. Each type has its own use and its own value.

Melody is inseparable from rhythm. Pure melody, that is, melody without rhythm, may be conceived in abstract theory; but in actual musical composition and performance, the tones of a melody invariably occur in a rhythmic movement of some sort. The rhythm may have little accent and no fixed metrical pattern, as exemplified in the Solesmes[1] interpretation of Gregorian chant; but in such a case, it is not that the melody lacks rhythm, but that the rhythmic movement is of a particular or unusual nature. Rhythmic movement of some type is so important to melody that it must be included in its definition. *Melody* is a pattern of related tones occurring in rhythmic succession.

The qualities of a good melody include *unity, emphasis,* and *coherence—* qualities necessary to the aesthetic value of any art form. A melody must be the complete statement of one musical idea; it must begin, continue, and come to a conclusion. The conclusion may be tentative and the statement may not be

---

[1] During the eighteenth and nineteenth centuries, the monks at the Benedictine Abbey at Solesmes, France, made a study of Gregorian chant. The interpretation based on their studies is now the official interpretation used by the Roman Catholic Church.

exhaustive, but without the feeling of completion and conclusion, the melody is weak and ineffective.

Emphasis in a melodic line means forward motion to a climactic point and on to a conclusion. It is this sense of movement, almost of urgency, that gives to the melody a real rather than a forced existence. Because it is one of the most subtle and least tangible of all musical qualities, emphasis in a melodic line illustrates the genius of the great composer and the pedestrian talent of the poor one. For all its subtlety, a few obvious matters may be pointed out. The melody should have only one climax in pitch, either high or low; the too frequent repetition of any single pitch or of any rhythmic value weakens the emphasis of a melody. A composer of talent, however, can rescue a seemingly impossible melody by changing it ever so slightly. The musical ear and the imagination are the true arbiters of quality.

The third quality, that of coherence, means that the melody must be heard and thought as a whole, not as unrelated segments. Coherence is affected by pitch level, by rhythmic construction, and by the key or keys implied. Extremely wide leaps should not divide a melodic line into separate sections. Similarly, rhythmic movement and implications of key should be such that the melody is not split into unrelated segments.

ANALYSIS OF IMPLIED HARMONY

The analysis of melody is principally concerned with harmony and form. Since form was discussed in Chapter 14, let us now examine the harmonic implications of a melodic line. A melody implies harmony because some successive notes outline chords, and because some notes are in strong, others in weak rhythmic positions. Melodic lines are made up of both chord tones and non-harmonic tones; the chord tones are usually in a position of rhythmic strength, so that the underlying harmony is discernible. Figure 17.1 shows a melody with an analysis of its harmonic implications. Notes connected by the same bracket are members of the same chord. Notice that all the tones of a chord do not have to be present in the melody for that chord to be implied. The only chords used in Figure 17.1 are the tonic, subdominant, and dominant, including the dominant seventh. It is often possible to harmonize simple melodies with only these principal chords of the key; more complex harmonization may also be used.

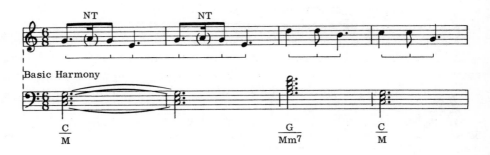

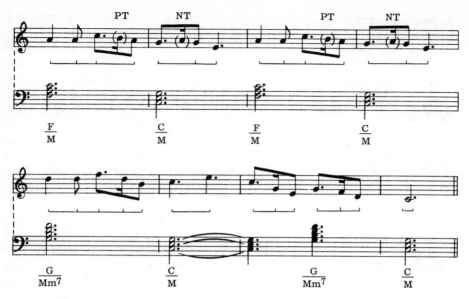

Figure 17.1. Harmonic Implications of the Melody of Silent Night

Melodic lines do not always imply harmony as obviously as this example does. Since it is sometimes difficult to determine which tones of a melody are non-harmonic and which are chord tones, a few practical suggestions may be helpful:

1. The first and last notes are usually chord tones.

2. Long notes are usually chord tones.

3. Notes immediately repeated are usually chord tones.

4. Notes that precede and follow a rest are usually chord tones.

Figure 17.2 shows other melodies that have clear harmonic backgrounds. Notice that in most cases the accented tones are chord members; non-harmonic tones are likely to be rhythmically weak.

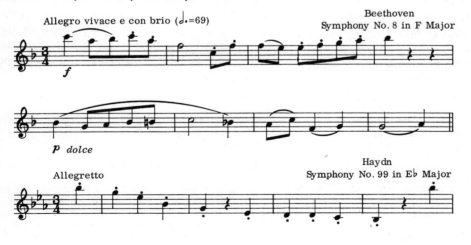

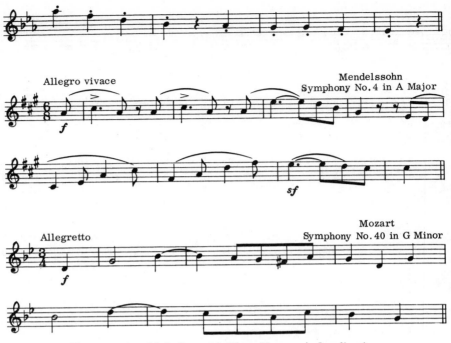

Figure 17.2. Melodies with Clear Harmonic Implications

MELODY TYPES

There are three basic types of melodies—*chant melodies, song melodies,* and *motivic melodies.* None of the three types is limited to a particular kind of music. Chant melody is found both in early Christian religious music and in Wagner's *Tristan und Isolde.* Motivic melody occurs in gospel songs as well as in symphonies of the classic period.

Chant melodies seem to move forward without interruption or repetition to a logical conclusion. Many of the beautiful melodies of Gregorian chant, also called *plainsong,* are of this type. Chant melodies have several characteristics: 1) they lack internal structure (*i.e.,* sections within a phrase); 2) they have a gently flowing rhythmic movement; 3) there is no regular pattern of phrase length; and 4) the harmonic implications, especially the cadence harmonies, are not obvious. Chant melodies may occur alone, or with an accompaniment that supplies a harmonic and rhythmic background. Each of the melodic phrases in Figure 17.3 (parts a,[2] b,[3] c,[4] and d[5]) is a chant melody.

---

[2] From *Plainsong for Schools* (Desclée et Cie., Tournai, Belgium), p. 1. Copyright 1933. Used by permission.

[3] Copyright 1912 by G. Schirmer, Inc. Copyright renewed 1939 by G. Schirmer, Inc. Used by permission.

[4] Copyright 1917 by G. Schirmer, Inc. Copyright renewed, International Copyright secured. Used by permission.

[5] Anglican chant has a special conventionalized notation in which the symbols do not represent actual rhythmic values. The first whole note of each phrase represents an indeterminate number of syllables, the number changing from verse to verse of the text. The half notes carry one syllable each and have approximately the time value of that syllable in ordinary speech. See *The Hymnal . . ., 1940* (New York: The Church Pension Fund, 1940), p. 697 f.

Figure 17.3. Chant Melodies

Chant melody depends largely on the melodic tendencies of different tones of the scale. Since the cadence of the chant melody must be achieved without strong harmonic implications, the feeling of conclusion must be brought about by the use of rhythm and the careful choice of active and rest tones. Chant melodies also have a limited pitch range; they could easily lose their coherence if wide leaps occurred without the unifying effect of harmonic and motivic materials. Not only do chants have more stepwise motion than other melodies, but most leaps are small; the occasional wide leap is followed by a change in direction of the melodic line.

When a chant melody has a text, the more important syllables come at the high points of the melody, or are emphasized by having more notes or longer notes than the syllables around them. Texts for chant melodies may be either prose or poetry, since the melody does not have a regular phrase structure. The position of the cadence is determined primarily by the length of each line of text.

Song melodies are clearly distinguishable from chant melodies. Song melody exhibits a regular pattern of phrase lengths and depends strongly on the harmony that the melody implies. The harmony of the cadence pattern is particularly evident. Phrases in a song melody are not easily divisible into smaller sections such as motives and semi-phrases, but seem to move in one uninterrupted flow from the beginning to the cadence. Song melodies are not limited to vocal music, but occur in instrumental music as well. Several song melodies are shown in Figure 17.4.

Song melodies, with their clear harmonic implications and regular phrase structures, are likely to be cast in the period or double period form, with a

Figure 17.4. Song Melodies

standard cadence at the end of each phrase. The regularity of the form makes such melodies more suited to poetical texts than to prose. Song melodies can also be used for instrumental music. These melodies make greater use of wide leaps than do chant melodies, but the leaps are normally made between notes in the same chord of the implied harmony. The harmony may be quite simple, as in a folk song, or it may aspire to something more complex, as in the art songs of the romantic period. Changes of harmony implied by a song melody usually occur at some point of accent; it is extremely rare that a chord starts in a position that is rhythmically weak if it is to continue through a point of accent.

The third type, *motivic melody*, shows a highly developed internal web of musical ideas, based on one or more motives. Since it is extremely difficult to build a phrase of nothing but motivic material, composers normally introduce some free material into it as well; this is used to connect different forms of the motive, or to bring the phrase to a proper cadence. A motive may be repeated literally (repetition); it may be repeated at a different pitch (sequence); or it may be varied in one of several ways. These include alteration of intervals in the motive, repetition of the rhythmic pattern, or inversion of the motive (in exact or modified form). The note values in the motive can also be halved or doubled, procedures called *diminution* and *augmentation*. Motivic melody has the regular phrase length and strong harmonic implications of song melody, but it adds to this a motivic structure within each phrase. Figure 17.5 shows three motivic melodies; others may be seen in Figure 14.1, on page 136.

Figure 17.5. Motivic Melodies

Melodic phrases may not fall clearly into any one of these categories of chant, song, or motivic structure. A phrase that at first seems to be of the song type may, upon closer examination, reveal a motivic structure. These descriptive categories, nevertheless, prove to be quite useful. None of these types of melody construction is, by its nature, superior to the other types. Each has its rightful place in the whole of music; each functions in its own way.

ESSENTIAL VOCABULARY

1. melody
2. unity
3. coherence
4. emphasis
5. chant melody
6. song melody
7. motivic melody
8. plainsong

9. repetition
10. sequence
11. interval alteration
12. rhythmic repetition
13. inversion
14. diminution
15. augmentation

ASSIGNMENTS

1. Write a chant melody to fit each of the following texts. Separate each text into several sections, and let each section constitute one phrase of the chant melody. The tonality of each melody should be clear.

a) Blessed is the man that hath not walked in the counsel of the ungodly, nor stood in the way of sinners, and hath not sat in the seat of the scornful.

b) The Lord is my shepherd; I shall not want.

---

[6] Reprinted from the Eulenberg Pocket Score of the complete *Scheherazade* with permission of C. F. Peters Corporation, New York, N.Y. 10016.

c) We hold these truths to be self-evident, that all men are created equal, that they are endowed by their Creator with certain unalienable Rights, that among these are Life, Liberty, and the pursuit of Happiness.

2. Write a song melody in period form for each of the following poetical excerpts. Provide a harmonic analysis to indicate the harmony implied by the melody.

a) Awake my soul and with the sun
   Thy daily stage of duty run.

b) O my love's like a red, red rose
   That's newly sprung in June.

c) She walks in beauty, like the night
   Of cloudness climes and starry skies.

d) I remember, I remember
   The house where I was born.

3. Write four motivic melodies in period form, each for a different instrument. Specify the instrument, and be sure to use the clef and range appropriate to it. Mark the basic motives, and provide a functional harmonic analysis.

4. Expand each of the motives in Figure 17.6 into a motivic melody in period form. Conclude with an authentic cadence. Provide a functional harmonic analysis.

Figure 17.6

18

Chord Choice
for Melodies

HARMONIZING A MELODY means choosing chords that are compatible with the melody itself. Chord tones in the melody should also be members of the chords chosen to accompany it. Melody tones that are not members of the underlying harmony will necessarily be non-harmonic tones. If a song melody or motivic melody is written in traditional style it will have a clearly implied harmonic background; it is assumed that students will be using this style. Each phrase of such music is based on a progression of chords that leads to a cadence. In the process of composition, the melody and the other textural elements grow out of this basic harmony. Sometimes the composer does this consciously, at other times unconsciously. In harmonizing a pre-existing melody, it is necessary to construct a suitable harmony from the chords implied by the melody itself.

HARMONIC RHYTHM

One of the questions that arises in choosing chords is how fast the harmony should change. Should every note have a new chord? Some pieces change chords rapidly, others change slowly. The rapidity with which chords change is known as *harmonic rhythm*. In Figure 18.1, the same melody is harmonized first with a chord change on almost every note, and then with several notes to each chord. The basic harmony, shown on the lower staff in the example, merely indicates the spelling of the chords to be used; it is not intended to show either the actual notes to be played or the proper spacing or arrangement of these chords. The difference in harmonic rhythm in these two harmonizations affects the nature of the music greatly. A rapid movement is achieved by infrequent changes of chord, whereas the use of many chord changes creates a slow, ponderous feeling in the melody.

Figure 18.1. *Different Harmonizations of the Same Tune*

In order to choose his chords, one should first assess the nature of the melody itself by hearing it. This may be done either by playing or singing it, or by thinking its sound. What chords are implied, and what is the key? Where are the cadence points, and what is the formal structure?

STEPS FOR A BEGINNER

Several distinct steps will help a beginner in choosing suitable chords to harmonize a melody:

1. *Decide on the cadence chords.* Each phrase of the music should end with one of the normal cadence patterns described in Chapter 12. The notes of the melody will determine which cadences are possible.

2. *Choose the first chord of each phrase.* The first phrase of a piece should establish the key immediately, by having a tonic chord on either the first note or the first accent. If there is a pickup note, it may be harmonized either with a tonic chord in root position, or with a dominant chord. The rest of the phrases offer more freedom of choice, but the first few chords should establish the key clearly by having a tonic or dominant chord, or both, near the beginning of the phrase.

3. *Choose the remaining chords.* Choose chords for the rest of the phrase that will maintain a normal chord progression[1] most of the time. Secondary resolutions, third relationships, or even irregular resolutions may be used, but these should not be as frequent as the primary resolution. Remember that frequent chord changes make music seem slow, and infrequent chord changes achieve a sense of faster movement. Chords should not change slowly in one measure and rapidly in the next. Chords may be repeated or held from a strong to a weak accent; chords are not repeated or held from a weak to a strong accent, except with pickup notes.

Students are often tempted to use certain chord progressions that do not follow a logical progression. The following progressions, which seem to be troublesome, should be avoided until the student is experienced in melody harmonization:

a) tonic to supertonic, unless followed by a major dominant chord;

b) major dominant to subdominant to tonic;

c) major dominant to supertonic to tonic;

d) supertonic to subdominant;

e) leading tone triad to subdominant.

Let us examine the melody in Figure 18.2, the first phrase of the famous German hymn *O Haupt voll Blut und Wunden*, in order to see some of the possibilities for harmonization.

Figure 18.2

This hymn is slow and stately, so a basic harmonic rhythm of one chord change to each quarter note would suit its style. Harmonized simply in C major, as in Figure 18.3, the phrase would end in an imperfect authentic cadence.

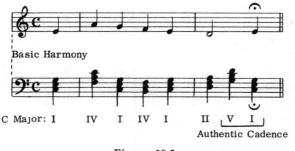

Figure 18.3

Other chords are possible in C major; moreover, this particular phrase may also be harmonized in A minor. An alternate harmonization in minor mode is shown in Figure 18.4, having a Phrygian cadence at the end of the phrase.

---

[1] See Chapters 8 and 10.

CHORD CHOICE FOR MELODIES   *171*

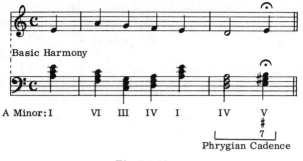

Basic Harmony

A Minor: I   VI   III   IV   I   IV   V
                                    ♯
                                    ‾7‾
                                Phrygian Cadence

Figure 18.4

Other melodies might have fewer chord changes in each phrase. In *Believe Me If All Those Endearing Young Charms,* Figure 18.5, chord changes occur only at points of relative accent. Except for the pickup notes at the beginning, no chord is held through an accent stronger than the one on which it begins.

Basic Harmony

D Major: I   IV   I   V   I
                                        Authentic Cadence

Figure 18.5

Whenever a melody is in a minor key, it is likely to contain tones that have been altered from the key signature of natural minor. If such tones are a part of the implied harmony, the chords used to harmonize them will also have to be altered. Such a situation occurs in Figure 18.6, taken from Bach's harmonization of the chorale tune *Herr, ich habe missgehandelt.*

Basic Harmony

A Minor: I   IV   V   IV   V⁷   I   II⁷ V   I
              ♯   ♯   ♯   ♯   ♯
              6   7   6   7   ‾7‾
                                        Authentic Cadence

Figure 18.6

The F♯ and G♯ in the melody are the Dorian sixth and the leading tone in the key of A minor, occurring not only in the melody, but also in the chords that support it. If there is more than one melodic line in the music, an altered tone in any of the melodies will affect the harmony in this way.

1. harmonic rhythm

2. basic harmony

ASSIGNMENTS

1. Copy the melodies in Figure 18.7 and choose chords with which to harmonize them, indicating the chords by a functional analysis. Mark all non-harmonic tones with parentheses. Carefully consider the harmonic rhythm before deciding on the chords. A fermata (⌢) indicates the end of each phrase.

Figure 18.7

19

Writing a Bass
Countermelody

ONE OF THE most common elements of musical texture is the *countermelody*, which was mentioned briefly in Chapter 16. A countermelody provides a contrasting part to the principal melodic idea. The art of writing one or more countermelodies is called *counterpoint*, one of the oldest of musical studies. Its name is derived from the Latin *punctus contra punctum*, meaning note against note, and the term dates back to the fourteenth century. Even in the twentieth century, counterpoint of a different sort is still one of the composer's basic skills.

Counterpoint involves at least two independent but related melodies, a principal melody and a countermelody. The relationship of the two depends upon the style of the music and the cultural tradition from which it derives. Counterpoint from different centuries sounds quite different, but regardless of style, the relationship of a melody and a countermelody is still called counterpoint.

MOTION BETWEEN MELODIC LINES

Two melodies performed at the same time can move in several ways. They can, for example, both go in the same direction—either higher or lower—at the same time; they can move in opposite directions; or one melody or voice can remain at the same pitch while the other moves. The different motions possible between two melodic parts are described by the following terms:

Similar motion
Parallel motion
Oblique motion
Contrary motion
Stationary voices

Similar motion occurs when two voices move in the same direction, either both going upward, or both going downward at the same time, as in Figure 19.1.

Figure 19.1

Parallel motion is a special kind of similar motion in which the voices simultaneously move the same interval in the same direction. With most intervals, it is customary to disregard interval quality and consider two voices to be in parallel motion if they move the same diatonic (*i.e.*, numerical) interval. The melodies in Figure 19.2 are considered to move in parallel motion, even though the voices move a different number of half steps.

Figure 19.2

When there is a fifth between the two voices, they are considered to move in parallel motion only if they move exactly the same number of half steps, that is, the same precise interval, quality included. In this special case, shown in Figure 19.3, a definite distinction is made between consecutive fifths in parallel motion and in similar motion.

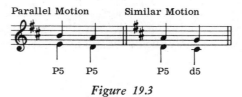

Figure 19.3

Oblique motion occurs when one of the two voices moves while the other remains stationary, as in Figure 19.4. The stationary voice may hold its note or it may repeat it.

Figure 19.4

Contrary motion occurs when two voices move in opposite directions at the same time. Figure 19.5 illustrates both contrary and oblique motion.

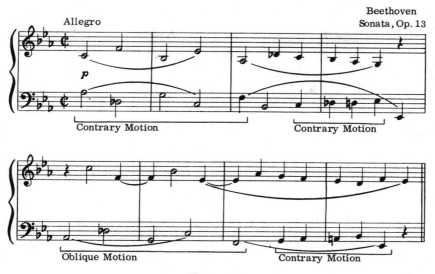

Figure 19.5

Stationary voices describes a condition in which neither of the two voices moves; both remain where they are. Students often mistakenly confuse stationary voices, marked with boxes in Figure 19.6, with parallel motion.[1]

Figure 19.6

A countermelody should provide adequate interest and contrast to the principal melody. Although related harmonically, the melodies should be melodically independent. Independence is achieved by rhythmic variety and through generous use of oblique and contrary motion between the two melodic lines. Parallel and similar motion weaken the independence of the countermelody. A few special kinds of motion tend so strongly to destroy the independence of the two melodies that the use of these motions has been forbidden in traditional harmony and counterpoint.

---

[1] The stationary fifths and stationary octaves shown are not forbidden in traditional harmony, although parallel motion between voices a perfect fifth or an octave apart is forbidden.

FORBIDDEN MOTION BETWEEN TWO VOICES

Consecutive perfect octaves and *consecutive perfect unisons*,[2] both shown in Figure 19.7, are forbidden between two independent voices, unless the voices are stationary.

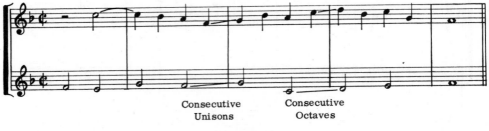

Consecutive
Unisons

Consecutive
Octaves

Figure 19.7

A distinction should be made between doubling a single melodic line at the octave or at the unison, as Beethoven has done in Figure 19.8, and having consecutive octaves or unisons between two different voice parts. The reinforcement of a single melodic line by octave or unison doubling is a common device in music for piano or for orchestra. Some pieces for orchestra, for instance, will have all the instruments playing the same melody; the result will be the doubling of the melody in several octaves at the same time. Still more common is doubling at the octaves by first and second violins or by violins and flute. In much early symphonic music the cellos and basses regularly played the same bass part in octaves, because the double-bass sounds an octave lower than the cellos when playing the same note. Such doubling of a single melodic line in octaves is quite acceptable.

Figure 19.8. Doubling of a Melodic Line at the Octave

---

[2] Sometimes called *parallel octaves, parallel unisons,* and *contrary octaves.*

Consecutive perfect fifths (also called *parallel fifths* and *contrary fifths*) are similarly forbidden, because these too destroy the independence of separate melodic lines. Consecutive fifths such as those in Figure 19.9 are forbidden whether there is parallel motion or contrary motion from one fifth to another; they are not forbidden when the voices are stationary.

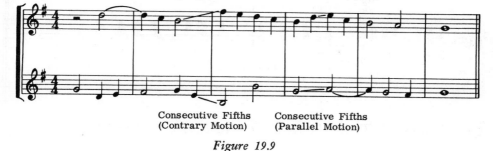

Consecutive Fifths   Consecutive Fifths
(Contrary Motion)   (Parallel Motion)

Figure 19.9

The presence of passing tones or other non-harmonic tones will not eliminate the bad sound of consecutive octaves, unisons, or fifths. On the other hand, the presence of such non-harmonic tones as those in Figure 19.10 may cause forbidden consecutive intervals where they would not otherwise occur.

Consecutive Fifths   Consecutive Fifths

Figure 19.10

Octave to unison and *unison to octave* create the same effect as consecutive octaves; this movement, shown in Figure 19.11, is therefore forbidden between two independent voices.

Octave to
Unison

Figure 19.11

Like doubling in octaves, the device of octave to unison or vice versa is sometimes used to reinforce a single melodic line, as occurs in the right hand in Figure 19.12. Since in this case the motion is not between two independent voices, the prohibition does not apply.

WRITING A BASS COUNTERMELODY   *179*

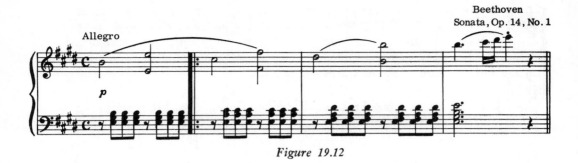

Figure 19.12

QUESTIONABLE MOTION BETWEEN TWO VOICES

Certain motions between voices that can cause an undesirable sound under one set of conditions may be quite acceptable under other conditions. In such cases the trained ear must finally decide the acceptability of the motion. The suggestions that follow are not strict rules to be applied under all circumstances; instead, their purpose is to guide the beginner until he develops the ability to discriminate between satisfactory and unsatisfactory sounds. The names of these questionable motions provide a useful vocabulary for discussion when they occur in composition or in analysis.

The *direct octave*, *direct fifth*, or *direct unison* (also called *hidden octaves*, *hidden fifths*, and *hidden unisons*) is an octave, fifth, or unison between two independent voices which is approached in similar motion. Such an approach to these intervals is not always undesirable, but it gives a bad sound if the upper of the two voices moves upward by leap, or if one of the notes of the direct octave, fifth, or unison is preceded by the seventh of a tetrad. The direct octave and the direct fifth are particularly noticeable when outer voices are involved. Several cases are shown in Figure 19.13.

Direct Unison
(not satisfactory)

Figure 19.13. Direct Octave, Direct Fifth, and Direct Unison

Overlapping occurs when one voice moves a greater interval toward another voice than their original interval apart. The identity of the two voices may be obscured, as if the melody had transferred from one voice to the other. Overlapping of only a half step is not objectionable.

Crossed voices occur if the lower of two voices sounds a note higher than that of the regular upper voice, or vice versa. Crossed voices are unsatisfactory if the crossing is wide enough or prolonged enough for the identity of the voices to be confused. Students should avoid crossed voices.

Similar fifths occur when two voices a fifth apart move in similar motion, but not parallel motion, to another fifth. Similar fifths are unsatisfactory if the outer voices move from a diminished to a perfect fifth. Two different examples are shown in Figure 19.14.

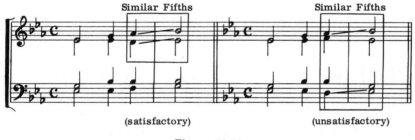

(satisfactory)   (unsatisfactory)

Figure 19.14

Cross relation is the presence, in different voices, of two different accidentals for the same note in close proximity, such as the F sharp and F natural in Figure 19.15. The cross relation is objectionable if the different accidentals are the result of an illogical progression, or if the two accidentals confuse the feeling of key.

Cross-relation

Figure 19.15

WRITING A BASS COUNTERMELODY   *181*

Consecutive dissonances, such as consecutive seconds or consecutive sevenths, are generally poor, like those in Figure 19.16, but they may occasionally occur if some of the notes involved are non-harmonic tones. Many factors affect the acceptability of consecutive dissonances—the amount of dissonance in the piece as a whole, the length of the dissonant notes, the register in which the dissonances occur, and their relation to the harmonic structure. Again, it is the trained ear that must judge the acceptability of the sound.

Figure 19.16

From this discussion of forbidden and questionable motions, it may be seen that three basic principles underlie any decision as to the desirability or undesirability of a specific kind of movement. One principle is that the melodic lines should be independent of each other. Any movement that destroys or weakens the melodic independence of either of the two voices should be avoided. Secondly, the melodic lines should be identifiable as continuous melodies. Motion that destroys or weakens melodic continuity or identity should be avoided. Thirdly, the harmonic progressions underlying the two melodies should be clear. Melodic movement that creates confusing or unpleasant harmonies should also be avoided.

BASS COUNTERMELODY

Skill in writing a bass countermelody is essential to a composer. Although it is possible to construct a bass countermelody by mechanically following rules, little skill in composition is developed until one learns to hear in his own mind the sound of the melody and countermelody together as they are being composed.

A bass countermelody implies the harmonic structure of a piece of music, but it must also be a continuous melodic line. The bass countermelody employs the following tonal material: the roots of all chords in the key except the leading tone triad; the thirds of all chords in the tonic, first, and second classifications; the seventh of any tetrads employed, and the principal non-harmonic tones (passing tones, neighboring tones, and the two-three suspension). Chord roots predominate; they are more frequent than chord thirds, and much more frequent than chord sevenths. The fifths of chords are not used in a bass line, except in a few special ways which are described in Chapter 22; they should be avoided for the present.

Bass lines rarely employ melodic intervals that are awkward or very large. Augmented intervals are particularly rare, since they are difficult to sing. Large intervals, such as the seventh or intervals larger than an octave, tend to destroy the continuous quality of the melody, so, except for the octave itself, they are little used. Even after a smaller leap such as a fourth, fifth, or sixth, the melody normally changes direction to maintain unity. Smooth, stepwise motion is highly desirable.

The melody and the bass countermelody will occasionally have the same note. Such doubling generally involves one of the principal tones of the key—tonic, dominant, or subdominant. Scale steps that have a strong tendency to resolve in a particular way are not doubled in both voices. Thus the leading tone, the seventh of a chord, and tones that are altered from the signature of the existing key are not doubled. For example, the Dorian sixth in a minor key is not doubled.

Whenever the seventh of a chord appears in the bass line it has a normal resolution, that is, it goes down by step to a chord tone in the next chord. Even tones that appear to be non-harmonic tones will follow this pattern of resolution if they happen to form the seventh of a chord.

It may be helpful to give a brief summary of this discussion in the form of instructions for the beginning student. It is assumed that, at this stage, the student can recognize and employ the dominant-seventh chord and all triads that employ only the diatonic tones of a key. (This includes the usual alternate tones of the minor scale, but excludes what is generally called chromatic alteration.) For the time being, tetrads other than the dominant seventh will be excluded, as will the use of chords in the second inversion, which is discussed in Chapter 22.

Before attempting to write a bass countermelody, a student should play the melody and choose chords for it, as explained in Chapter 18. Once the chord progression has been thoroughly checked, the bass countermelody may be begun.

BEGINNER'S INSTRUCTIONS FOR WRITING A BASS COUNTERMELODY

1. Make up a bass line that consists only of the roots, thirds, and sevenths of the chords that have been chosen, plus the principal non-harmonic tones. Chord roots should predominate. Chord sevenths, which are not frequent, must resolve properly. For the present, do not put the fifth of the chord in the bass.

2. Start with a root position tonic chord on either the first note or the first accent. The bass line for cadence chords should employ chord roots most of the time.

3. Listen in your mind for the relationship between the principal melody and the bass. There should be no forbidden motion between the two voices; questionable motion should be used with great care, so as to avoid an unsatisfactory sound. Doubling of the same tone in both voices should occur only with the principal tones of the scale; it should not occur with altered tones or tendency tones.

4. Notes longer than those around them, or longer than the basic rhythmic movement of the piece, should be considered chord tones, not non-harmonic tones. Notes before or after a rest, or at the beginning or end of a phrase, should be chord tones.

5. Check the sound of what you have written by singing each of the two parts separately without accompaniment, and also by playing the two parts together or by hearing them in your mind. Make any corrections necessary to improve the sound of what you have written.

ESSENTIAL VOCABULARY

General
1. countermelody
2. counterpoint
3. bass countermelody
4. melody doubling

Motions between two voices
5. similar motion
6. parallel motion
7. oblique motion
8. contrary motion
9. stationary voices

Forbidden motions between two voices
10. consecutive perfect octaves
11. parallel octaves
12. contrary octaves
13. consecutive perfect unisons
14. parallel unisons
15. consecutive perfect fifths

16. parallel fifths
17. contrary fifths
18. octave to unison, or unison to octave

Questionable motions between two voices
19. direct octave
20. direct fifth
21. direct unison
22. hidden fifths
23. hidden octaves
24. hidden unisons
25. overlapping
26. crossed voices
27. similar fifths
28. cross relation
29. consecutive dissonances

ASSIGNMENTS

1. Identify and label each of the motions between melody and bass countermelody in Figure 19.17.

Bach
Meinen Jesum lass' ich nicht, weil

Gibbons
O Lord Increase My Faith

Figure 19.17

2. Identify, label, and briefly explain all cases of poor writing in Figure 19.18.

Figure 19.18

3. Provide a bass countermelody for each of the melodies in Figure 19.19. Use the harmony indicated. Name each cadence and label all non-harmonic tones in both the melody and bass countermelody.

WRITING A BASS COUNTERMELODY   *185*

Figure 19.19

4. Choose harmony for each of the chorale melodies in Figure 19.20; write a bass countermelody to fit the harmony you have chosen.

Figure 19.20

5. Choose harmony for each of the folk-song melodies in Figure 19.21; write a bass countermelody to fit the harmony you have chosen.

Figure 19.21

6. Choose harmony and write bass lines for the melodies in Figure 19.22, which are chosen from orchestral music.

Figure 19.22

20

Writing in
Four Voices

ONE OF THE standard patterns of musical texture consists of four voices—soprano, alto, tenor, and bass. The Lutheran hymn tunes, or *chorales,* that were harmonized by Johann Sebastian Bach have long been considered the finest examples of good four-voice writing. Not only are they rich in harmony, but all the voices have strong melodic qualities. The study of four-voice writing is usually based on these brilliant examples. In this texture the soprano and bass are called *outer voices.* The soprano has the melody, and the bass, as usual, serves its dual purpose of acting as a countermelody and implying the harmony. The *inner voices,* alto and tenor, serve principally to complete the harmony implied by the outer voices; but from time to time, these inner voices act as additional countermelodies as well. Writing music in four voices is often called *part writing.*

The outer and inner voices of four-voice writing are different in style. The counterpoint between the outer voices involves considerable movement. The inner voices, on the other hand, tend to progress much more smoothly. In many cases the alto and tenor move to the nearest chord tone possible. Leaps in inner voices tend to be small.

The process of harmonizing a melody in four voices consists of three main steps—choosing a progression of chords suitable for the melody, writing an appropriate bass countermelody, and adding the inner voices. Choosing a suitable chord progression was discussed in Chapter 18. Writing an appropriate bass countermelody was explained in Chapter 19. We are now concerned with the procedure of completing the four-voice texture by the addition of the two inner voices. The increased number of parts forces us to consider the range and spacing of voices, the necessary doubling of chord tones, and the avoidance of forbidden motion between any two of the four voices. We must also try to maintain a melodic quality in the inner voices.

RANGES OF THE VOICES

Bach intended the chorales to be sung, so the four parts are limited to the style and range of the human voice. The ranges of voices in a chorus are given in Figure 20.1; the black notes represent possible extremes of range that might or might not be satisfactory, depending upon the abilities of the singers. Trained soloists, however, might well sing beyond these limits. All notes within the range of a particular voice cannot be sung with the same ease. If the tenor part, for instance, stays near the top of its range too long, it will begin to sound strained and uncomfortable. Each of the voices should therefore be balanced around the middle of its range, without staying very high or very low for too long at a time.

Soprano   Alto   Tenor   Bass

Figure 20.1.   Ranges of Choral Voices

SPACING OF THE FOUR VOICES

In addition to the matter of individual voice ranges, there are limitations in the *spacing* of voices. If a single voice is too far from its neighboring parts, good intonation will be difficult to maintain. As a practical guide, there should not be more than an octave between any two adjacent upper voices—soprano to alto or alto to tenor. The distance between the tenor and bass may be greater than an octave, but each voice must, of course, stay within its own range.

Some experimentation in spacing the notes of chords in four voices will show that two basic chord structures are possible with the spacing limits stated above. A chord is in *close structure* if the three upper parts are close enough together that the soprano and tenor are an octave or less apart. The chord is in *open structure* if the soprano is more than an octave from the tenor. Figure 20.2 shows several chords arranged in both close and open structure.

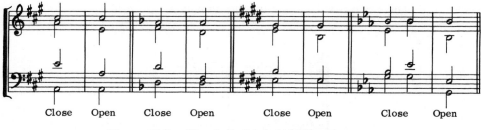

Close   Open   Close   Open   Close   Open   Close   Open

Figure 20.2.   Chords in Open and Close Structure

PRINCIPLES OF DOUBLING

If a three-note chord is played or sung by more than three voices, at least one tone of the triad must be *doubled;* that is, it must be played or sung by more than one of the voice parts. In a chord for full orchestra, all tones of the chord will be played by several instruments. Composers' doubling useage is affected by a chord's function, its inversion, the spacing of the chord, the quality of sound desired, and the melodic movement of individual voices. The principal tones of the key—tonic, dominant, and subdominant tones—are doubled more often than lesser degrees of the scale. With major and minor triads, doubling the chord fifth results in a smooth, almost glassy sound; a doubled third creates a sharp, pungent quality that is particularly noticeable in a major triad; but doubling the root gives a sensation of strength and solidity.

PATTERNS OF DOUBLING IN FOUR VOICES

In four voices it is necessary to double one of the three tones of the triad. Although composers vary in their doubling practices, the doubling patterns found in the Bach chorales will serve as a guide to good usage. Regular doubling patterns, those that are used most of the time, are discussed in four sections: major and minor triads, diminished triads, augmented triads, and dominant seventh chords.

In major and minor triads, the tone to be doubled is determined by the inversion, as in Figure 20.3. In root position, the root is doubled; in first inversion, the soprano is doubled; in second inversion, the bass note is doubled.[1]

Figure 20.3

The diminished triad is almost always used in first inversion, and it is customary to double the third, so that the third occurs in the bass and in one other voice. If the chord fifth happens to be in the soprano, either the third or the fifth may be doubled. These two possible doublings are shown in Figure 20.4.

Figure 20.4

---

[1] See Chapter 22.

The rarely used augmented triad always has a doubled bass note, whether in root position or in first inversion.[2] It is not used in the second inversion.

The dominant seventh chord, having four tones, would seem to present no doubling problem, but this is not the case. If the dominant seventh has its usual resolution to the tonic, and if both chords are in root position, the fifth is customarily omitted from either the tonic or the dominant seventh, as shown in Figure 20.5. An extra root replaces the omitted fifth in either case. In inverted forms, the dominant seventh usually contains all four tones without doubling.

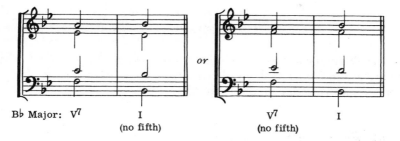

or

Bb Major: V⁷   I
              (no fifth)

V⁷   I
(no fifth)

Figure 20.5

IRREGULAR DOUBLINGS

Doubling patterns that do not follow the usages described above are called *irregular doublings*. It may be necessary to double irregularly in order to avoid forbidden motion between individual voices. In such cases one of the principal tones of the key—tonic, dominant, or subdominant—should be doubled. Some chord progressions require irregular doubling. When moving from one first-inversion chord to another, as in Figure 20.6, care is necessary to avoid forbidden motion; irregular doubling is a frequent means of escape.

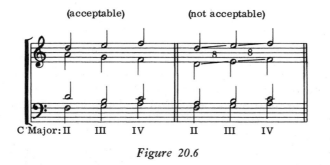

(acceptable)   (not acceptable)

C Major: II   III   IV   II   III   IV

Figure 20.6

Root position chords on adjacent steps of the scale usually require irregular doubling. One procedure is to double the third in one of the two chords, as is done in Figure 20.7. The third of a dominant chord must not be doubled because it is the leading tone.

---

[2] See Chapter 22.

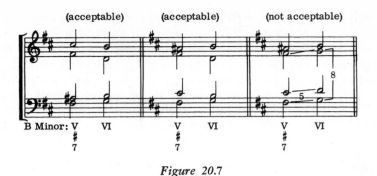

Figure 20.7

Minor triads frequently use a doubled third instead of regular doubling. This is particularly noticeable with the II, III, and VI chords in major keys. Chords with doubled thirds are shown in Figure 20.8.

Figure 20.8

Some tones tend so strongly to move in a specific direction that doubling them causes problems of voice leading. It is therefore customary to prohibit the doubling of the leading tone, of the seventh of a chord, or of any tone altered from the signature of the existing key; this includes the Dorian sixth and the leading tone in a minor key.

On rare occasions, irregular doubling will cause the omission of one member of a chord. The fifth is the tone commonly left out, so chords may occasionally occur that consist of three roots and one third, or of two roots and two thirds. The third of a chord is almost never omitted.

Good doubling usage is summarized in the guidelines given below; they provide a basic grammar of chord doubling which students should follow strictly. Students should remember that these guidelines are based on customary usage for four voices. If there are more than four voices, the composer must judge what effect doubling certain tones will have on the sound of the chord.

DOUBLING GUIDELINES: WHAT TO DO

1. With major and minor triads, double the root in root position, the soprano in first inversion, and the bass note in second inversion.[3]

2. With diminished triads, double the third; if the fifth is in the soprano, double either the third or the fifth.

3. With augmented triads, double the bass note.

4. With a root position dominant seventh chord that is followed by a root position tonic, omit the fifth from either chord and add another root. In other progressions, or if the dominant seventh is inverted, do not omit or double tones.

5. Irregular doubling may be necessary when chord roots are a second or a third apart, or when moving from one first inversion to another.

DOUBLING GUIDELINES: WHAT NOT TO DO

1. Do not omit the third of any chord.

2. Do not double an active tone. This includes the leading tone, the seventh of any chord, or any tone altered from the existing key, such as the Dorian sixth.

ADDING THE INNER VOICES

Let us assume that you have before you a soprano melody, and that a suitable harmonic progression has been chosen. Moreover, a bass countermelody has been written to fit that melody and harmony. How are the inner parts added? Let us remember that the alto and tenor parts should complete the harmony implied by the outer voices; they should also add their own melodic interest.

Because it is important that the sound of the melody and bass be thoroughly familiar, these two parts should be played, sung, or thought until there is no doubt about their sound. The inner parts may then be added, preferably in several steps.

Step I. Choose the structure. If the soprano and bass are near each other, close structure will be necessary; if the outer parts are widely spaced, either close or open structure is possible. Once chosen, the structure should not be changed without good reason; a change in the spacing of the outer voices, for instance, may suggest a change in structure. Structure is most easily changed in one of four situations: 1) at a repeated chord, 2) when approaching or leaving a chord in first inversion, 3) after a cadence, or 4) when one of the upper voices leaps as much as a fourth.

---

[3] See Chapter 22.

Step II. Make up the inner voices from the tones of the chords chosen and from non-harmonic tones. Non-harmonic tones should not obscure the harmony. The inner voices should be as smooth melodically as possible, but each chord should have the proper spacing and doubling. There must be no forbidden motion between any of the voices. The seventh of any chord should not be approached by a downward leap, and each chord seventh must resolve downward to a chord tone in the next chord.

Step III. Check your work. First, sing each part to be sure that none is awkward or unmusical. Next, check each chord for proper spacing and doubling. Finally, check each pair of voices (soprano and bass, alto and bass, tenor and bass, soprano and tenor, alto and tenor, alto and soprano) note by note to see if there is any forbidden motion or any questionable motion that is undesirable.

ESSENTIAL VOCABULARY

1. four-voice writing
2. chorales
3. outer voices
4. inner voices
5. part writing
6. range
7. spacing
8. close structure
9. open structure
10. doubling
11. irregular doubling

ASSIGNMENTS

1. Write the following major triads in four voices in open structure. Be sure to use correct doubling and spacing.

	ROOT	INVERSION	SOPRANO POS.
a)	C	Root	5
b)	C♯	Second	3
c)	E	Second	8
d)	A♭	Root	3
e)	G♯	Second	3
f)	D	First	8
g)	G	Root	3
h)	B	First	5
i)	E	Root	5
j)	C♭	Root	3
k)	E♭	First	8
l)	B♭	Second	8
m)	C	First	3
n)	A♯	Root	5
o)	G	Second	3
p)	D♯	First	8
q)	A	First	5
r)	E♭	First	5
s)	B	Second	3
t)	C♯	First	5

2. Write the following minor triads in four voices in close structure. Be sure to use correct doubling and spacing.

	ROOT	INVERSION	SOPRANO POS.
a)	B♭	Second	8
b)	F♯	First	3
c)	A♭	First	3
d)	F♯	Root	5
e)	B♭	Root	5
f)	F	Second	3
g)	D	First	8
h)	G♭	First	8
i)	A	First	5
j)	F♯	Second	3
k)	B♭	First	5
l)	F	Second	8
m)	C♯	First	8
n)	B	Root	3
o)	E♭	First	5
p)	A	Root	8
q)	D♯	Root	5
r)	G	Second	5
s)	A♯	First	5
t)	F	Root	3

3. Rewrite Figure 20.9 in close structure in the same key. Do not change the soprano or the bass.

Figure 20.9

4. Rewrite Figure 20.10 in open structure in the same key; move the bass melody down one octave. Do not change the soprano.

Figure 20.10

5. In the exercises in Figure 20.11 the soprano, the bass, and the harmony are given. Add the inner voices.

WRITING IN FOUR VOICES   *197*

Figure 20.11

6. In the exercises in Figure 20.12 the soprano melody and the harmony are given. Add a bass countermelody and the inner voices.

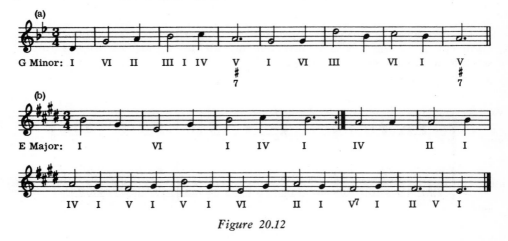

Figure 20.12

7. In the exercises in Figure 20.13 the melody and bass countermelody are given. Choose a harmony which the soprano and bass imply and add the inner voices.

Figure 20.13

8. Write a bass and add alto and tenor parts for the melodies in Assignment 3 in Chapter 19, page 185.

9. Write the melodies in Assignment 4 in Chapter 19, page 186, in four-voice harmony.

10. Arrange a familiar folk-song tune for four-voice chorus without accompaniment. Keep the harmony similar enough to the original so that the tune is easily recognizable. Some suggested tunes are:

a) *Believe Me, If All Those Endearing Young Charms*

b) *Drink to Me Only with Thine Eyes*

c) *Columbia the Gem of the Ocean*

d) *Auld Lang Syne*

11. Write a four-voice hymn tune for any Common Meter hymn. A *Common Meter hymn* has a four-line stanza, with eight syllables in the first and third lines and six syllables in the second and fourth lines, such as the following:

> O God, our Help in ages past,
> Our Hope for years to come,
> Our Shelter from the stormy blast,
> And our eternal Home.

WRITING IN FOUR VOICES 199

21

Figured Bass

In THE BAROQUE period of music history, which dates roughly from 1600 to 1750, habits of musical performance were quite different from present-day custom. Musical scores rarely had keyboard accompaniments that were written out in full form. Instead, the keyboard performer played from an abbreviated score that consisted only of the melody and a *thorough-bass*, also called a *basso continuo*. In some cases, especially when an orchestra was involved, even the principal melody was omitted, so that only the bass countermelody was written out for the keyboard performer. He then had to improvise a complete keyboard accompaniment from the bass melody; this was called *realizing a bass*.

In order to indicate the intended harmony more clearly, the bass part was often *figured*, meaning that numerals and accidentals were written above or below the bass part to show what intervals should accompany each note. The bass figuration was sometimes fragmentary, sometimes full, and often entirely lacking, but its presence made the performer's task much easier and insured that what he played would fit the intended harmony.

Bass figuration was thus a system of shorthand musical notation that indicated a harmonic structure to the performer. If this seems inadequate to modern musicians, it must be remembered that the composer himself was often at the keyboard. Moreover, musicians at that time were trained from childhood in the skill of realizing a thorough-bass. It should also be pointed out that the practice of playing from a figured bass does not differ greatly from present-day dance band usage, in which the pianist more often than not plays from a *lead sheet*, which has only the melody and an indication of the proper chord.

When a bass is fully figured, the figuration forms a system of intervallic analysis quite separate from a functional analysis or a root/quality analysis. Each of the three systems gives some information about the harmonic structure to which it refers. In the study of harmony, it is useful to write both the functional analysis and a bass figuration. In traditional usage, the bass figuration is written just above or just below the bass line. It will be more convenient for us to write it just below the bass line, with the functional analysis below that, as shown in Figure. 21.1.[1]

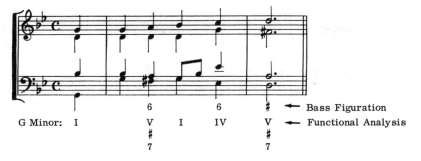

Figure 21.1. Dual System of Analysis

PRINCIPLES OF BASS FIGURATION

When a bass is figured, each numeral indicates an interval above the bass note. The interval is in accord with the written key signature, unless some change is shown in the figuration. When a note in a figured bass has no written figuration, the numerals 8, 5, and 3 are understood, representing the intervals of the octave, fifth, and third above the bass note. Any combination of these intervals is possible; which tones are actually present is determined by the doubling usage and by the melodic movement of individual voices. The spacing and the doubling of the voices are not shown in the figuration.

In Figure 21.2 the bass notes have no written figuration. Notice, for instance, that the first five chords have the same bass note, but different arrangements of the upper voices, each of which forms the interval of either octave, fifth, or third above the bass note.

Figure 21.2. Bass Notes without Written Figuration

. If a written number six appears in the figured bass, a sixth is used instead of the fifth that would be understood if no number were written. A written four

---

[1] Some theorists combine an abbreviated bass figuration with the functional analysis in order to indicate chord inversion. A first inversion tonic or dominant chord is thus analyzed as I_6 or V_6; second inversions are indicated by a six and a four, as in I_4^6. No objection is raised to this procedure, but it is quite different from historical figured bass usage. The combined analysis should be thought of as an enlargement of functional analysis, rather than as a bass figuration.

similarly shows that a fourth occurs instead of a third. In each pair of chords in Figure 21.3, the written figure has replaced one that is understood.

Figure 21.3

A written figure seven sometimes replaces the octave that would be understood and sometimes shows that a seventh is used in addition to the octave. Both cases are shown in Figure 21.4.

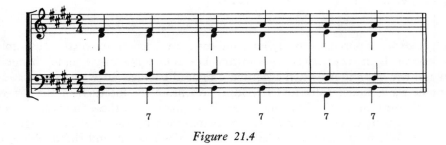

Figure 21.4

Other numbers in a figured bass indicate the presence of the indicated intervals, whether due to inversion of a chord or to non-harmonic tones. Occasionally, even the numbers eight, five, and three are written out for purposes of clarity, or to indicate the voice leading of a particular melodic line, as shown in Figure 21.5.

Figure 21.5

Quite elaborate patterns of figuration, such as that in Figure 21.6, occur when it is necessary to indicate the individual movements of several voices. As in other situations, the numbers refer to intervals above the bass note. A dash shows that a particular figure is retained over a sustained or repeated bass note.

Figure 21.6

Because of the practical, day-to-day use of bass figuration in the seventeenth and eighteenth centuries, a number of abbreviations developed. The figuration $\frac{4}{2}$, and sometimes 2, are abbreviated forms of $\frac{6}{2}$; the figuration $\frac{4}{3}$ is a shortened form of $\frac{6}{4}$.

ACCIDENTALS IN A FIGURED BASS

Any accidental in an upper part that differs from the written key signature is indicated in the figuration; changes in the accidentals that occur in the bass line itself are not shown. An accidental that affects the third above the bass note is shown by the accidental alone, as in Figure 21.7.

Figure 21.7

If an interval above the bass other than the third is to be raised one half step from the spelling indicated by the signature, the raised interval is shown by a figure with a diagonal line through it, as shown in Figure 21.8.

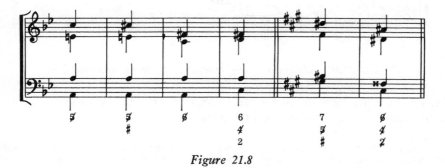

Figure 21.8

FIGURED BASS   *203*

If any other change in accidental is to take place, the new accidental and the number are both written, with the accidental to the left, as is done in Figure 21.9.

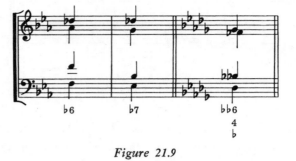

Figure 21.9

NON-HARMONIC TONES IN THE BASS

If a bass line contains non-harmonic tones, these notes are customarily unfigured. In illustrating a proper realization of a bass, Johann David Heinichen, for instance, writing in 1728, left the passing tones in the bass line unfigured, as shown in Figure 21.10.[2]

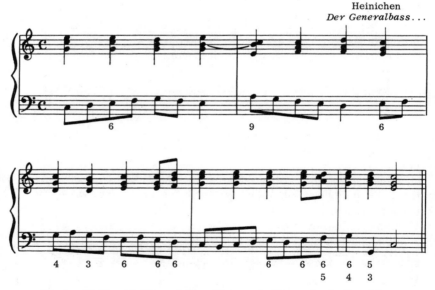

Figure 21.10.   Unfigured Non-Harmonic Tones in the Bass Line

Bach, on the other hand, often figured non-harmonic tones, as in Figure 21.11, so that the harmonic implications would be all the more clear.

[2] Quoted in George J. Buelow, *Thorough-Bass Accompaniment According to Johann David Heinichen* (Berkeley, Los Angeles: University of California Press, 1966), p. 94.

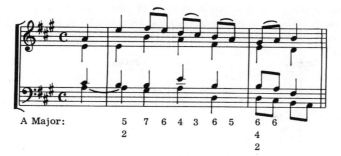

A Major: 5   7 6 4 3 6 5   6 6
             2   4
                                              2

Figure 21.11. Figured Non-Harmonic Tones in the Bass Line

REALIZING A FIGURED BASS

In order to make it possible for modern players to perform thorough-bass music, it is usually necessary to write out a realization of the bass part. The pianist or harpsichordist plays the original bass part with the left hand, sometimes doubling it at the octave below. The right hand generally plays smoothly moving chords in three voices. The accompaniment is not supposed to double the principal melody. The accompanying parts thus resemble the four-voice writing of the chorale style and utilize the principles described in Chapter 20.

ESSENTIAL VOCABULARY

1. thorough-bass
2. *basso continuo*

3. figured bass
4. lead sheet

ASSIGNMENTS

1. In the key of A major, what figuration would be used to indicate:
a) I chord in first inversion?
b) IV chord in second inversion?
c) V^7 chord in root position?
d) V^7 chord in third inversion?
e) II chord in first inversion?
f) V^7 chord in first inversion?
g) V chord with the note A as a suspension?

2. In the key of B minor, what figuration would be used to indicate:
a) V chord in root position?
$$\frac{\sharp}{7}$$

b) IV chord in first inversion?
$$\frac{\sharp}{6}$$

c) V^7 chord in root position?
$$\frac{\sharp}{7}$$

d) VII chord in first inversion?

$$\begin{array}{c}\sharp\\7\end{array}$$

e) II chord in first inversion?

f) V⁷ chord in third inversion?

$$\begin{array}{c}\sharp\\7\end{array}$$

g) I chord in second inversion?

h) I chord in root position?

$$\begin{array}{c}\sharp\\3\end{array}$$

3. Assume that the figured bass notes in Figure 21.12 represent unrelated chords. Complete the chords in four voices, with proper doubling and spacing. Use any soprano position, and either close or open structure. Give a root/quality analysis. Do not attempt a functional analysis because isolated chords cannot establish a key.

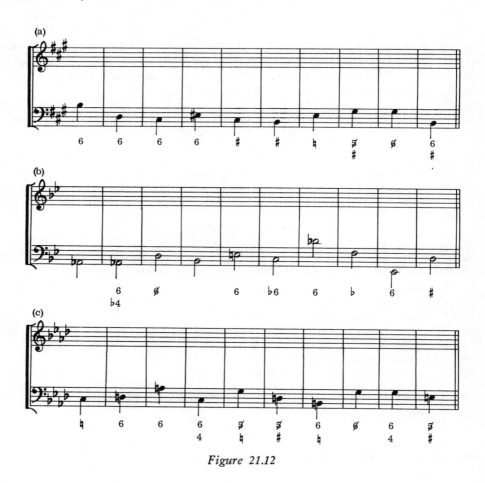

Figure 21.12

4. Figure 21.13 is a song from Bach's *Schemelli Gesangbuch*. The upper part is a vocal melody; the lower part is a thorough-bass that is figured. Realize the bass in four voices without doubling the principal melody. Avoid forbidden motion between any two voices.

Figure 21.13

22

Voice Leading Chords

ALTHOUGH MOST CHORDS can be employed in a number of different progressions, some are limited in their use to specific idioms of melodic movement or chord progression. The most common of these limited chords are second inversions; others include the first inversion of the mediant and the leading tone triad. All such chords may be described as *voice leading chords*. A voice leading chord is the result of the melodic movement of individual voices rather than a basic change of harmony. Although it usually creates a logical progression, the primary function of a voice leading chord is to allow smooth melodic movement and at the same time to maintain a pleasant consonant sound. Most voice leading chords are the incidental result of non-harmonic tones in several voices.

Consider the two bracketed chords in Figure 22.1. The chord at A is a voice leading chord; it is preceded and followed by dominant harmony; the only digression from the dominant sound is caused by passing tones in the alto and bass. This smooth melodic movement creates a combination of sounds that could be analyzed as a VI⁷, but the chord exists only because of the non-harmonic movement. The chord at B, on the other hand, is not a voice leading chord, for it is more the result of an essential harmony change than of mere melodic movement. Notice that the bass leaps, and that the two chords before and after it are different.

Figure 22.1. Nature of Voice Leading Chords

In one sense, all chords have some voice leading qualities because they are best connected by smooth melodic motion. On the other hand, the most obvious voice leading chord also involves harmonic change, however slight. There is consequently no sharp line of division between the basic chords that make up the harmonic progression and voice leading chords which result from smooth melodic lines. In spite of this ambiguity, the concept of a voice leading chord helps us understand and explain some common chords that act in an uncommon way.

In order to understand the nature of voice leading chords better, let us look at a tonic chord, followed by its own first inversion, as shown in Figure 22.2. If a passing tone is added in the soprano or in the bass, or in both together, the harmony will remain unchanged.

Figure 22.2. Chord Progression with Non-Harmonic Tones

If, in addition to the two passing tones, a lower neighbor is added in the alto, the essential chord movement still has not changed. The tones on the second beat now form a voice leading chord, however, for they may now be analyzed as a V^7 chord in the second inversion. A close examination will reveal that this voice leading form of the V^7 differs from regular dominant seventh chords. The chord seventh, for instance, is not resolved in downward motion as is usual; moreover, there are similar fifths between alto and soprano that would not be acceptable in most other progressions. All this makes us suspicious of this chord as a harmonic entity. Examination of a large quantity of music, however, would show that this voice leading form of the V^7 chord is employed in the same way with such regularity that this usage is by now quite commonly accepted. Most voice leading chords occur in idiomatic patterns of this sort.

Voice leading chords may be recognized by several characteristics. They occur largely where there is stepwise motion, with melodic patterns that resemble the common non-harmonic tones. Voice leading chords occur between two strong, independent chords, often between two forms of the same chord. Moreover, the voice leading chord seems to be preparatory or transitory in relation to the adjacent chords upon which it is dependent.

It should be obvious that the dividing line between functional chords and voice leading chords is shadowy. A vertical structure that is a functional chord in one situation may, with different rhythm or spacing of voices, be a voice leading chord. Duration and purpose affect the voice leading quality of chords. If a voice leading chord is prolonged enough to lose its significance as a melodic intermediary between other chords, it loses its voice leading quality and takes on a functional aspect. Almost any voice leading chord becomes a functional chord if sufficiently extended in time. Each case, however, must be judged separately on the basis of tempo, harmonic context, textural pattern, especially the importance of melodic movement, and other such matters of style.

FUNCTIONAL ANALYSIS OF VOICE LEADING CHORDS

Because voice leading chords are part chord and part non-harmonic material, the usual functional analysis does not always contribute to our understanding of the chord. A functional analysis assumes that the chord analyzed has a firm relation to the tonality of the music; that is the reason it is analyzed in terms of its numerical relationship to the tonic. A voice leading chord, being the result of melodic movement, does not bear as strong a relationship to the tonic as to the two chords adjacent to it. That relationship is not primarily harmonic, but is a melodic relationship, voice by voice. For this reason, if a functional analysis is stated for a voice leading chord, the analysis should be placed in parentheses, or otherwise differentiated from the analysis of ordinary functional chords.

THE PASSING GROUP

One group of voice leading chords is characterized by a bass note that has the melodic pattern of a passing tone. This group includes the *passing six-four*, the *passing six-three*, and the *passing six-four-three*. If assigned a functional analysis, these three chords would be, in order, V in second inversion, VII in first inversion, and V⁷ in second inversion. These usually occur between the root position and first inversion of the same chord, most often a tonic chord. Figure 22.3 shows the various patterns in which the chords of the passing group may occur.

(a) Passing Six-Four

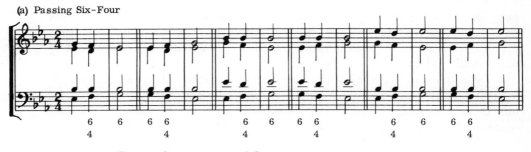

Which pattern is used depends largely on the melodic movement of the upper voices. The chords have all been shown in the same key so that their similarity would be more obvious. The supertonic scale step is the bass note in each of these chords; in every instance the bass note is doubled.

(b) Passing Six-Four-Three

(c) Passing Six-Three

Figure 22.3.   Passing Six-Four, Passing Six-Four-Three, and Passing Six-Three Chords

The analysis of these chords could take any of three forms, which are shown in Figure 22.4 for the passing six-four-three. The analysis at (a) treats all the moving parts as non-harmonic tones, ignoring the chord that results from them. At (b) the structure on beat two is recognized as a voice leading chord, but it is not assigned a chord function. The procedure at (c) treats the structure as a second inversion dominant seventh, but the voice leading nature of the chord is recognized by putting the functional analysis in parentheses. The analysis at (b) is recommended in most cases.

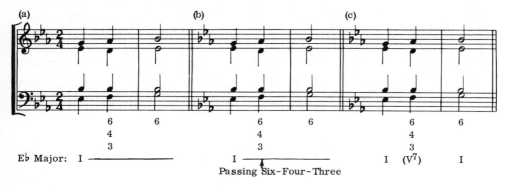

Figure 22.4.   Three Forms of Analysis for Voice Leading Chords

Occasionally the chords in the passing group fail to move on to their usual resolution, but return instead to the same chord that preceded them. These unresolved passing chords are not essentially different from those shown above.

THE ORNAMENTAL SIX-FOUR AND ORNAMENTAL SIX-THREE

The voice leading chords known as the *ornamental six-four* and the *ornamental six-three* are characterized by an unchanging bass note, which may be either sustained or repeated. In the six-four, two of the upper voices move in a neighboring tone pattern; in the six-three, only one voice is involved. Figure 22.5 shows the ornamental six-four in the first phrase of *Silent Night*.

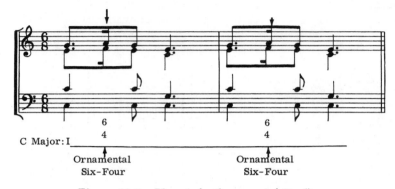

Figure 22.5. Use of the Ornamental Six-Four

The ornamental six-four usually exists in tonic harmony, with the tonic note in the bass; occasionally an ornamental six-four will be found over a dominant bass. The ornamental six-three usually has the dominant note as the bass tone.

In keyboard music, the ornamental six-four is sometimes prolonged over several beats, as shown in the excerpt from Mozart's Sonata in C major (K. 545), in Figure 22.6.

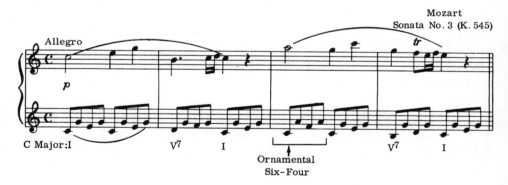

Figure 22.6. Ornamental Six-Four in Instrumental Music

THE CADENTIAL GROUP

Another group of voice leading chords—and a very important group—is found commonly, but not exclusively, in the preparation of a cadence. The most familiar of these chords is the *cadential six-four,* but the *cadential six-three* is not in-frequent. Each of these chords occurs on an accent just before the dominant chord in an authentic or deceptive cadence. The authentic cadence pattern in its simplest form is shown at (a) in Figure 22.7; a deceptive cadence would be identical, except for the final chord. Figure 22.7 also shows a number of variations in this pattern which may be made without an essential change in the basic harmony. At (b) a suspension has been introduced in the alto. The pattern at (c) has the suspended note in the soprano. The addition of two non-harmonic tones, as at (d), makes this structure look suspiciously like our old friend the tonic chord. Nevertheless, the doubling of the dominant bass note assures us that, for all its deceptive appearance, this is really a dominant chord with two non-harmonic tones.

Figure 22.7. *Voice Leading Chords of the Cadential Group*

Just as with the passing family of voice leading chords, alternate analyses of the cadential six-four and the cadential six-three are possible. If a chord function other than the dominant is assigned to these chords, such an analysis should be put in parentheses, as shown in Figure 22.8.

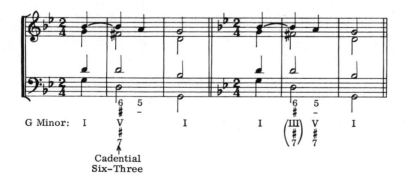

Figure 22.8. Alternate Analyses of Cadential Six-Four and Cadential Six-Three

These particular voice leading chords, especially the cadential six-four, have been in use so long, and are now so common, that little attention is paid to the manner in which the non-harmonic tones of the chord are approached. The resolution, however, follows a regular pattern in which the sixth and the fourth above the bass resolve downward to a fifth and a third. In the concertos of the classical period, the cadenza is preceded by a cadential six-four, with the resolution coming at the end of the unaccompanied solo passage.

Prolongation of the Cadential Six-Four

The familiarity of the cadential six-four has led to great freedom in its use. Occasionally the chord is prolonged with melodic movement in the upper voices. Such usage is particularly common in nineteenth century hymn tunes such as *What a Friend*, the last line of which is shown in Figure 22.9. In the final cadence, which occupies the last two measures, the six-four is prolonged, with some vacillation between the six-four and five-three structures over an unchanging bass note. The same chord function, which is essentially dominant, is protracted through the entire measure.

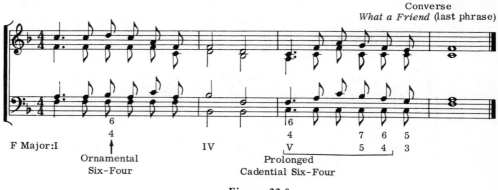

Figure 22.9

In earlier music, the six-four and six-three both appeared in a prolongation of the dominant function, such as that shown in Figure 22.10. The next to last measure has a dominant function throughout; in succession there are a cadential six-three, a cadential six-four, and a dominant chord with a suspension.

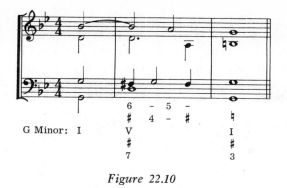

G Minor: I   V   I

Figure 22.10

Special Problems with the Cadential Six-Three

There is considerable uncertainty about the proper functional analysis of the chord which contains a sixth and a third above a dominant bass note. It is sometimes considered a first inversion of the mediant triad; a closer look, however, will show that it acts exactly like a dominant chord. The simplest form of the chord in both modes is shown in Figure 22.11. The chord frequently resolves

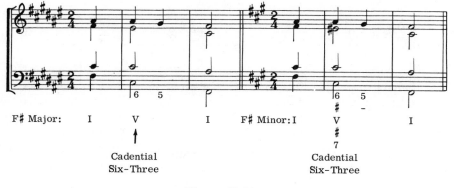

F♯ Major: I   V   I   F♯ Minor: I   V   I

Cadential   Cadential
Six-Three   Six-Three

Figure 22.11

deceptively, both in cadences and within the body of a phrase, as in Figure 22.12. Since the submediant chord is often preceded by the mediant, the deceptive res-

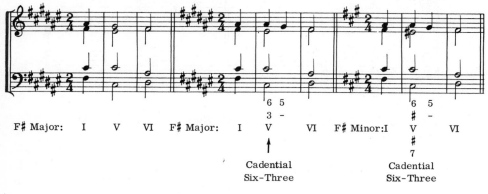

F♯ Major: I   V   VI   F♯ Major: I   V   VI   F♯ Minor: I   V   VI

Cadential   Cadential
Six-Three   Six-Three

Figure 22.12

VOICE LEADING CHORDS   215

olution of the cadential six-three resembles the regular harmonic step from fourth down to third level.[1] The similarity is particularly strong when the cadential six-three resolves directly to the submediant, as in Figure 22.13, without the usual explicit form of the dominant in between.

One other chord in the cadential group, the *cadential seven-six-three*, confirms the dominant function of the cadential six-three. Because the notes of the cadential

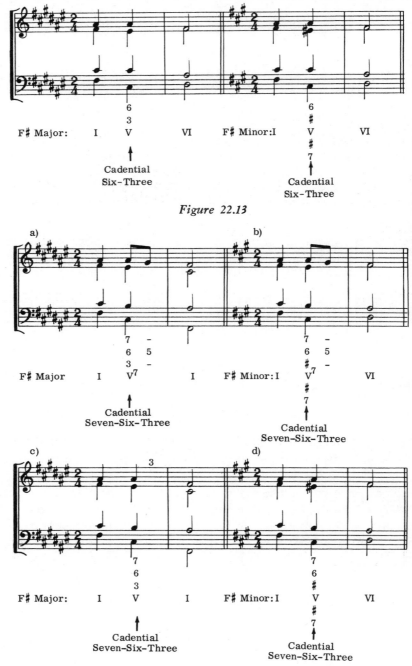

Figure 22.13

Figure 22.14.   The Cadential Seven-Six-Three

_____

[1] See Chapters 8 and 10.

seven-six-three spell neither a mediant nor a dominant seventh chord, its function must be determined by its use, which is identical to that of the dominant seventh. The cadential six-three is so similar that it too must be considered to have dominant, not mediant, function. The cadential seven-six-three is most often followed by an explicit dominant seventh, as at (a) and (b) in Figure 22.14. Late nineteenth century composers, however, sometimes resolved it directly to the tonic in an authentic cadence, or directly to the submediant in a deceptive cadence. These direct resolutions are shown at (c) and (d).

OTHER USES OF THE SECOND INVERSION

There are several uses of the second inversion other than those already described. The *arpeggiated six-four* occurs when the bass has an arpeggiated figure without a change of harmony. It is frequently used in keyboard music, but is not common in vocal music. Figure 22.15 shows a typical use of the arpeggiated six-four.

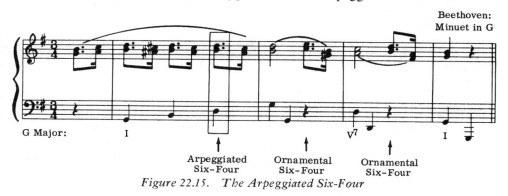

Figure 22.15. The Arpeggiated Six-Four

The *preparatory six-four* is a dominant triad in second inversion that is followed immediately by the root position of the chord. If the dominant chord is a tetrad, the chord becomes a preparatory *six-four-three*. Figure 22.16 shows the use of the preparatory six-four-three as it occurs in the first phrase of "Onward Christian Soldiers," set to the tune *St. Gertrude*.

The same tune uses the second inversion in another way that has no commonly accepted name. At the beginning of the refrain of the hymn, the bass

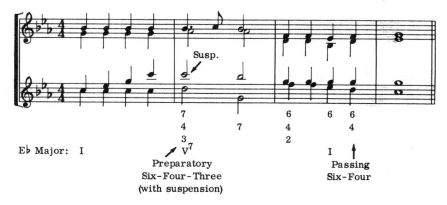

Figure 22.16. The Preparatory Six-Four-Three

moves back and forth from the root to the fifth of the tonic chord, and then from fifth to root of the dominant chord. This rocking or alternating bass is particularly characteristic of marches and of dance music. This is shown in Figure 22.17.

Figure 22.17.   *The Six-Four in an Alternating Bass*

The arpeggiated six-four, preparatory six-four, and the rocking bass figure are essentially instrumental idioms; they occur in vocal music only because of instrumental influence.

VOICE LEADING ASPECTS OF THE LEADING TONE TRIAD

The leading tone triad in both major and minor has some of the qualities of a voice leading chord and of a functional chord. This diminished triad is approached and left smoothly, as in the passing six-three, Figure 22.18, which has already been described. The leading tone triad utilizes this same smoothness in other

Figure 22.18

progressions as well. Compare those in Figure 22.19.

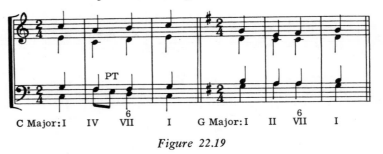

Figure 22.19

Bach commonly employs the leading tone triad in one idiomatic progression where the motion is not so smooth. In this situation, the chord acts more functionally, for the resolution of the chord requires a wide leap in one upper voice, usually the tenor, as in Figure 22.20. If the inner parts are high, this progression will allow them to stay in a comfortable range by shifting from close to open structure.

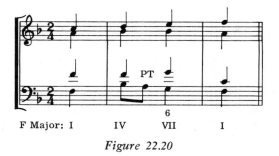

F Major: I   IV   VII   I

Figure 22.20

Let us recall that voice leading chords differ from other chords, in that they are the result of smooth melodic movement rather than basic harmony changes. No positive separation is possible between basic chord changes and voice leading chords, but the latter are recognized by the presence of stepwise melodic movement resembling non-harmonic tones, by the strength or similarity of the two adjacent chords, and by the transitory nature of the voice leading chord.

The most numerous voice leading chords are the so-called second inversions of the principal triads and the dominant seventh. The leading tone triad and the chord often called a first inversion of the mediant are also common voice leading chords.

ESSENTIAL VOCABULARY

1. voice leading chords
2. passing six-four
3. passing six-three
4. passing six-four-three
5. ornamental six-four
6. ornamental six-three
7. cadential six-four
8. cadential six-three
9. prolonged cadential six-four
10. cadential seven-six-three
11. arpeggiated six-four
12. preparatory six-four
13. preparatory six-four-three

ASSIGNMENTS

1. Analyze the excerpts from hymn tunes in Figure 22.21. Mark with brackets and name all voice leading chords. Label all non-harmonic tones that are not part of a voice leading chord.

Figure 22.21

2. Analyze each of the excerpts from Bach chorales in Figure 22.22. Mark with brackets and name all voice leading chords. Label all non-harmonic tones that are not part of a voice leading chord.

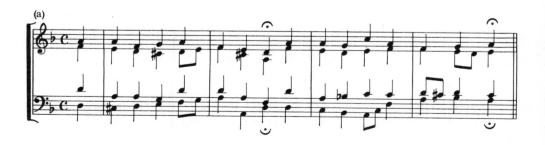

Figure 22.22

3. Copy from a hymnal and analyze the hymn tunes with the following tune names. Mark with brackets and name all voice leading chords. Label all non-harmonic tones that are not part of a voice leading chord.

a) *America*
b) *St. Catherine*
c) *Coronation*
d) *Regent Square*
e) *Christmas*
f) *Cwm Rhondda*
g) *Trinity* (Italian Hymn)

4. Add alto and tenor parts to Figure 22.23. Make a functional analysis. Mark with brackets and label all voice leading chords. Name all non-harmonic tones that are not part of a voice leading chord.

Figure 22.23

23

Subordinate
Non-Harmonic Tones

THE PRINCIPAL NON-HARMONIC tones were discussed in Chapter 13; these included the passing tone, the neighboring tone, and the suspension. There also are some subordinate non-harmonic tones that occur less frequently and in more limited situations. The circumstances in which these non-harmonic tones are used are as important as their definitions.

THE APPOGGIATURA

An *appoggiatura* (app.) is a non-harmonic tone that is approached by leap and left by step,[1] such as the soprano note D in Figure 23.1.

---

[1] Two definitions of the appoggiatura as a non-harmonic tone are in common use in the United States. The definition used in this book is the more common of the two. Some theorists, however, consider any accented non-harmonic tone an appoggiatura if it is resolved by step. By the latter definition, accented passing tones and accented neighboring tones would be considered appoggiaturas. For a discussion of both viewpoints, see George Thaddeus Jones, *Symbols Used in Music Analysis* (Washington, D.C.: The Catholic University of America, 1964), pp. 316–320. The word *appoggiatura* also means a melodic ornament or a grace note, frequently used in the baroque and classical eras. The use of the appoggiatura as a non-harmonic tone should not be confused with its use as an ornament, although the two are similar in origin.

Figure 23.1

An appoggiatura is usually in a prominent melodic voice. Because an appoggiatura may sometimes be used without its usual preparation, it may follow a rest or begin a musical phrase, as in the beginning of Mozart's G minor Symphony, shown in Figure 23.2.

Figure 23.2

The appoggiatura is usually as long as its resolution; Wagner and other romantic composers frequently employed appoggiaturas that were much longer than their tones of resolution, as in the last measure of Figure 23.3.

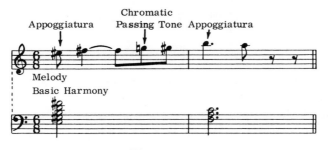

Figure 23.3

THE ANTICIPATION

An *anticipation* (ant.) is a non-harmonic tone that is approached by step and left by repetition or holding, as indicated by the arrow in Figure 23.4.

Although the anticipation may occur anywhere in a piece, it is most often found just before the end of a phrase. Approached either from above or below, the anticipation is rhythmically weaker than its preparation or resolution. Two or more anticipations may occur at the same time. If there is only one anticipation, it is nearly always in the uppermost voice.

SUBORDINATE NON-HARMONIC TONES   *223*

Figure 23.4

Infrequently, composers have used an anticipation to prepare some other non-harmonic tone, such as an appoggiatura; irregular usage such as this is limited, however, to the principal melodic voice.

THE ESCAPE TONE

An *escape tone* (E.T.) is a non-harmonic tone that is approached by step and left by leap, as in Figure 23.5.

Figure 23.5

The escape tone is nearly always in the most important melodic line, usually in the uppermost voice. It is commonly approached by upward step and left by downward leap. The escape tone is also called an *échappée*.

THE PEDAL POINT

A *pedal point* (ped.) is a non-harmonic tone that is approached by holding or by repetition and is left by holding or repetition, as the bass line in Figure 23.6.

The pedal point is usually a tonic or dominant tone in the bass part. Beginning and ending as a chord tone, it is held long enough for the harmony to change while it is being sustained. If it should be in an upper part, it is called an *inverted pedal point*. The term *pedal point* is often shortened simply to *pedal;* the term *organ point* is also used.

Figure 23.6

CHANGING TONES

Changing tones are a pair of successive non-harmonic tones a third apart, which resolve by step to a chord tone, like those in Figure 23.7. The pair of non-harmonic tones is often approached by step as well.

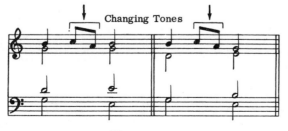

Figure 23.7

Changing tones occur most often in the principal melody line or the uppermost voice. They may be thought of as the combination of two neighboring tones, or of an escape tone and an appoggiatura.

It is possible to find rare instances in which composers have used non-harmonic material for which no consistent nomenclature has been established. One case is shown in Figure 23.8. Students should avoid such usage.

Figure 23.8

ESSENTIAL VOCABULARY

1. subordinate non-harmonic tones
2. appoggiatura
3. anticipation
4. escape tone
5. échappée

6. pedal point
7. inverted pedal point
8. pedal
9. organ point
10. changing tones

ASSIGNMENTS

1. Make a root/quality analysis of the excerpts in Figure 23.9; do not attempt a functional analysis. Mark with parentheses and label all non-harmonic tones.

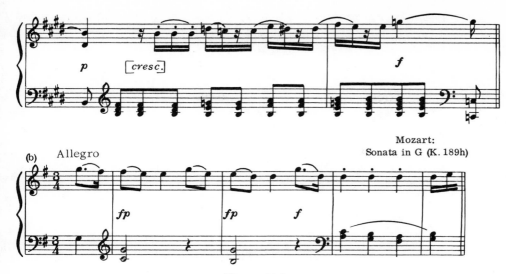

Mozart:
Sonata in G (K. 189h)

(b) Allegro

Figure 23.9

2. Find three examples in pieces of music of each of the following non-harmonic tones. Copy out the measure in which the non-harmonic tone occurs, along with the measure that precedes and follows it.

    a) appoggiatura
    b) anticipation
    c) escape tone
    d) pedal point
    e) changing tones

24

Accompaniment as

an Element of

Musical Texture

IN CHAPTER 16, the principal elements of musical texture were listed as melody, countermelody, and accompaniment. In the chapters that followed, we investigated the nature of a melody and the construction of a countermelody, especially one that occurs in the bass. We have also studied that particular combination of textural elements known as four-voice writing. It is now time for a closer look at the structure of an accompaniment.

In common usage, the word *accompaniment* signifies all that goes on in a piece of music except its principal melody. Many times the word refers to the entire piano part of a song for voice and piano, or the orchestral portion of a work for voice and orchestra. The same use of the word can be applied to accompanied pieces for various solo instruments. Analysis of the piano or orchestral portions of such music will reveal that the accompaniment actually includes several elements of musical texture. The principal melody, for instance, may be in the uppermost voice. There may be a clear countermelody in the bass, or possibly in another voice as well. For our purposes here we are concerned only with that element of the musical texture that is purely accompanimental, excluding the main melody or any countermelodies that may be present.

In order that we may more clearly distinguish between accompaniment in its general sense and accompaniment in its meaning as a single element of musical texture, let us look at Figure 24.1, which is an excerpt from Beethoven's song *Mignon* (Op. 75, No. 1). The part for the right hand is essentially the vocal melody, with some harmonic inner voices added. The left hand plays arpeggiated chords, but the bottom notes of the triplet patterns state a bass countermelody.

The other textural element—the triplet pattern itself—serves to establish a rhythmic and harmonic background for the principal melody. This pattern, exclusive of the melody and countermelody, is what constitutes the accompanimental element in the texture of the song.

Figure 24.1.   Accompaniment for Piano

In this chapter we need to examine some of the different ways of writing an accompaniment—using the word in the sense of a single element of musical texture. We shall therefore exclude from our present discussion other textural elements that are often used in writing a keyboard or orchestral part; they will be discussed in Chapter 25.

The nature of an accompaniment is greatly affected by the instrument or instruments that play it. If it is conceived for piano, it depends on the sustaining action of the damper pedal. Accompaniments for organ have longer held notes because the sound stops as soon as the finger is lifted. String accompaniments frequently employ rapidly repeated tones that are easily played with a bow. Moreover, an accompaniment must be subordinate to the principal musical idea. It should support and complement the main melody, but it should not overshadow it. Let us first look at some patterns of accompanimental texture that occur in the songs of Mozart, Beethoven, Schubert, and Schumann. These excerpts will show the most common means of using chords in a rhythmic pattern.

SUSTAINED CHORD ACCOMPANIMENT

One of the simplest accompaniments consists of sustained chords. Such an accompaniment is primarily harmonic, contributing very little to the rhythmic interest of the music. Figure 24.2 is typical of an accompaniment of sustained chords. At measure five, the piano part begins to play the melody as well as the accompanimental chords. Other examples may be seen in Figures 16.9 to 16.11 in Chapter 16.

Figure 24.2. Sustained Chord Accompaniment

REPEATED CHORD ACCOMPANIMENT

If the chords are repeated in a regular rhythm, they provide a pulse that establishes the tempo and movement of the music. Figure 24.3 is an excerpt from Beethoven's *Die Ehre Gottes aus Natur*. The chords are repeated in quarter notes, with very smooth voice leading when the chord changes.

Figure 24.3. *Repeated Chord Accompaniment*

The repeated chords in Figure 24.4 occur in *Die Lotosblume* by Schumann; however, the total chord structure is more complex. The top notes of the chords sound the principal melody, and the bass is a definite countermelody. In all, there are three textural elements in this excerpt—melody, countermelody, and an accompaniment of repeated chords.

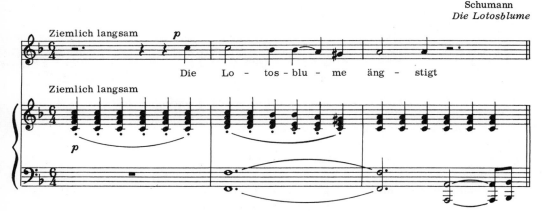

Figure 24.4. *Repeated Chord Accompaniment*

BROKEN CHORD ACCOMPANIMENT

An accompaniment of repeated chords may be fitted into any of several rhythmic patterns by breaking the chords into sections. This avoids the heavy quality of repeated chords and is easier to play on a keyboard instrument. The broken chords may be quite simple, as in Figure 24.5, or quite complicated, as in Figure 24.6.

ACCOMPANIMENT AS AN ELEMENT OF MUSICAL TEXTURE   *231*

Figure 24.5. Simple Broken Chord Accompaniment

Figure 24.6. Complex Broken Chord Accompaniment

ARPEGGIATED ACCOMPANIMENT

In addition to broken chords, composers have also used arpeggios and that particularly characteristic figure of eighteenth century music known as the *Alberti bass*. Arpeggios may be in the lower voices, as frequently employed by Chopin (Figure 24.7), or in the upper voices, as in Figure 24.8. Occasionally, non-harmonic tones will also appear in the arpeggiated figure. Accompaniments such as these depend on the sustaining action of the modern piano for their harmonic richness; they are less satisfactory on the organ.

Figure 24.7. Arpeggiated Accompaniment in the Left Hand

Mozart
An Chloe (K. 524)

Allegretto

Wenn die   Lieb' aus dei - nen   blau - en,   hel - len,

Allegretto

Figure 24.8. Arpeggiated Accompaniment in the Right Hand

ALBERTI BASS

The Alberti bass in Figure 24.9 differs from the arpeggiated figures because of its constant alternation of an upper chord tone with the bass note. Lying conveniently under the hand, it does not require the technical skill needed for extended arpeggio patterns. The Alberti configuration is idiomatic for keyboard music, and it is rarely found in other performance media. Mozart, Haydn, and Beethoven utilized the Alberti bass in much of their music for the piano.

Mozart
Sonata, K. 545

Andante

Figure 24.9. Alberti Bass Accompaniment

"UM-PAH-PAH" ACCOMPANIMENT

The strong rhythmic feeling of marches or dances is obtained by breaking the chordal structure into an accented bass note followed by the remaining voices of the chord, played alternately and repeated over and over. This provides the "um-pah" figure for marching bands and the "um-pah-pah" that characterizes the waltz and other dances. Both binary and ternary versions are often used in song accompaniments, such as that in Figure 24.10. The left hand is played on the accent and the right hand is played on the weaker parts of the beat. In this case, the lower voice, although broken by the accompanimental rhythm, still forms a bass countermelody in addition to providing the accent for the accompaniment.

Figure 24.10. "Um-pah" Accompaniment

Figure 24.11 is a segment of the famous "Waltz of the Flowers" from the *Nutcracker Suite* of Tchaikovsky. After the accompanimental rhythm is clearly established by the lower strings, the horns play the principal melody and some harmony notes as well. Accompaniments of this type are characteristic of the waltz.

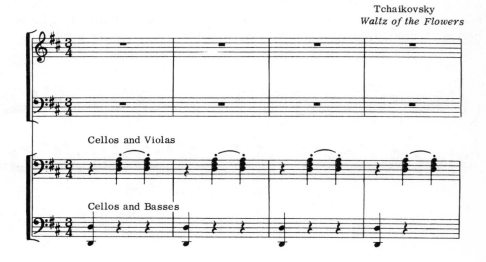

Figure 24.11. "Um-pah-pah" Accompaniment

ACCOMPANIMENT AS A PART OF THE WHOLE

Composers have generally been careful to see that the chords in the accompaniment, whether broken, arpeggiated, or merely repeated, do not create problems due to forbidden motion or poor doubling. The spacing of the accompanying chords should be such that the chord third or chord seventh does not occur simultaneously in both the melody and the accompaniment, or in a bass countermelody and the accompaniment.

Most composers treat the chord tones of accompanying chords as if they were continuous melodic voices that move along smoothly. The voice leading in Figure 24.12 shows the care that composers use to maintain good voice leading in accompanying chords.

The density of tones in the accompanying chords is primarily affected by the general loudness. Chords in soft passages have fewer, more widely spaced tones. Loud chords have many tones spaced close enough together so that they can be played with strength. Attention should also be given to the register in which the accompanying chords are played. Heaviness results from chords in a low

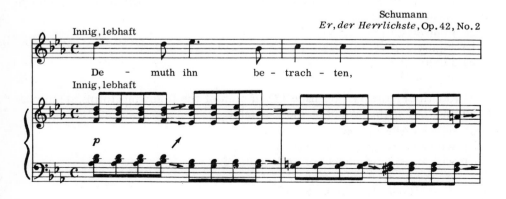

Figure 24.12. Voice Leading in Accompanying Chords

register, lightness from chords in a high register. As in so many other situations, the ear of the composer and of the performer must be the judge of what is proper.

It is rare that a composer maintains the same accompanimental pattern for an entire song. Changes in the pattern are significant devices for achieving variety or change of expression within a musical work.

ESSENTIAL VOCABULARY

1. accompaniment (general sense)
2. accompaniment (textural sense)
3. sustained chord accompaniment
4. repeated chord accompaniment
5. broken chord accompaniment
6. arpeggiated accompaniment
7. Alberti bass
8. "um-pah-pah" accompaniment

ASSIGNMENTS

1. Write accompanying piano parts for the melodies in:
a) Figure 3.4 on page 27
b) Figure 3.7 on page 31

2. Rewrite the music in Figure 5.16 on page 68 in compound triple meter so that the melody will have an accompaniment of arpeggiated chords.

3. Write a different style of accompaniment for each of the following musical examples in this chapter:
a) Figure 24.2
b) Figure 24.5
c) Figure 24.8
d) Figure 24.10

4. Rewrite Figure 14.3 on page 137 in each of the following forms. Transpose to another key if this would be more suitable.
a) with an Alberti bass accompaniment
b) with an arpeggiated chord accompaniment
c) with an accompaniment of broken chords

5. Discuss in a brief paper the style of accompaniment used in two songs by one of the following composers:

a) Ludwig van Beethoven
b) Franz Schubert
c) Robert Schumann
d) Robert Franz

25

Other Elements of
Musical Texture

MUSICAL TEXTURE WAS defined in Chapter 16 as the arrangement of musical ideas that occur at the same time.

It should be pointed out, however, that musical theorists are in wide disagreement about the nature of musical texture and how it should be analyzed. Formerly, theorists assumed that musical texture was either homophonic, that is, having one melody; or it was polyphonic, composed of several melodies. Homophonic music was assumed to be primarily harmonic, while polyphonic music was considered to be contrapuntal. Unfortunately, much music is not exclusively one type or the other.

The principal elements of texture that make up music are melody, countermelody, and accompaniment, but these are not the only textural elements that composers have used. In order to understand the structure of music better, let us now examine other possible elements of musical texture. These include *melodic doubling, melodic broderie, melodic outlining, elaboration, ostinato, extended pedal point, chordal motive,* and *reinforcement*.

MELODIC DOUBLING

It is common practice for a melody or countermelody to be doubled in a second instrument or in a different register. Octave doublings like those in Figure 25.1 (see Figure 19.8 also) are so common that they are likely to escape our notice. As pointed out in the section on part writing, doubling a single melodic line at the octave does not constitute a forbidden motion. The prohibition against consecutive octaves applies only to successive octaves between two independent melodic lines.

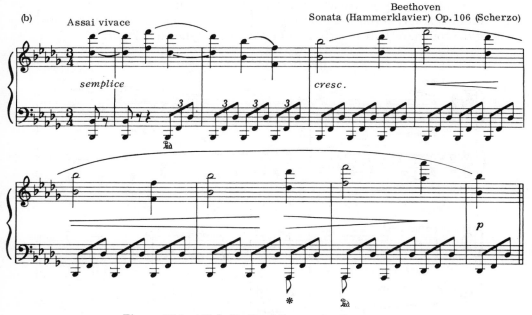

Figure 25.1. Melodic Doubling at the Octave

Doublings at the third and at the sixth (Figure 25.2) are also quite common. In most music from the classic and romantic periods, the melody is doubled at a diatonic interval, using the scale tones of the same key.

OTHER ELEMENTS OF MUSICAL TEXTURE   *239*

Figure 25.2. *Melodic Doubling at the Third and Sixth*

As the pattern of strong key feeling weakened in the latter part of the nine-teenth century, chromatic doubling became more common, such as the doubling of the countermelody in Debussy's *Le petit nègre*,[1] shown in Figure 25.3.

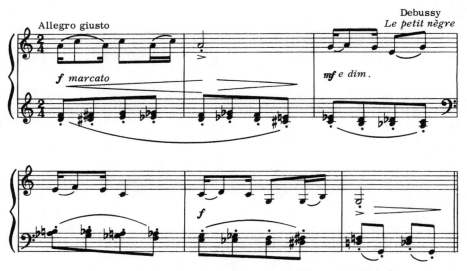

Figure 25.3. *Melodic Doubling of a Chromatic Melody*

In more recent music, such melodic doubling has been employed at other inter-vals, including the second, seventh, fifth, and fourth. A melody doubled at the sixth and fourth below, and a countermelody doubled at the octave are the prin-cipal constituents of this section of Bartók's *Music for String Instruments, Percus-sion, and Celesta*,[2] shown in Figure 25.4.

---

[1] Copyright by Alphonse Leduc & Co., 175, rue Saint-Honore, Paris Ier, owners and publishers.

[2] *Music for String Instruments, Percussion, and Celesta*. Copyright 1937 by Universal Edition; Renewed 1964. Copyright and Renewal Assigned to Boosey and Hawkes, Inc. for the U.S.A. Reprinted by permission of Boosey and Hawkes, Inc. for the territory of U.S.A. Reprinted by permission of Universal Edition for all other countries of the world.

Melody

Countermelody

Pedal Point

Figure 25.4.   Melodic Doubling as a Principal Compositional Method

MELODIC BRODERIE

In addition to simple doubling such as this, a melodic line may occur simultaneously in both its usual form and in an ornamented form. This textural element is called *broderie*, from the French word for embroidery. This compositional device is particularly important in Oriental music, but it also occurs more often in our own music than we sometimes realize. A notable example occurs in Schumann's song *Jasminenstrauch*, shown in Figure 25.5. The right hand of the piano part weaves a sixteenth-note pattern around the vocal melody.

Figure 25.5. Melodic Broderie

Mozart employed the same technique in his G major Sonata for Piano (K. 189h), a portion of which is shown in Figure 25.6. The left-hand melody, which is doubled at the octave, is also played in the right hand with a *broderie* of sixteenth notes.

Figure 25.6. Melodic Broderie *in a Piece for Piano*

MELODIC OUTLINING

The musical effect opposite to *broderie* is for one voice or instrument to *outline* the melody played by another. Figure 25.7 shows the principal melody of the last movement of Mozart's Symphony No. 40 in the violin part. The flute and oboe, in turn, outline the violin melody by playing only the principal notes. The device of outlining often occurs when low instruments such as the double-bass or the tuba outline a melody being played by higher instruments.

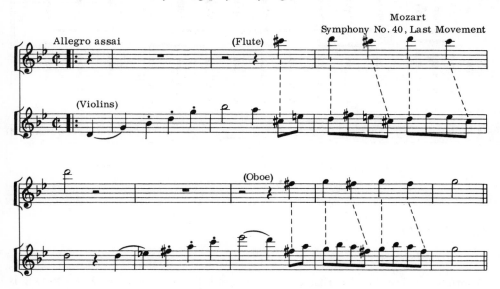

Figure 25.7. Melodic Outlining

ELABORATION

Composers also employ a kind of decoration that is unrelated to a particular melodic line; this kind of decoration, called *elaboration*, applies to the whole musical fabric, like frosting on a cake. Elaboration usually takes the form of arpeggios or scales superimposed on the main structure of melody, countermelody, and accompaniment. A typical example occurs in Wagner's Overture to *Tannhäuser*, part of which is shown in Figure 25.8; the violins weave a delicate figure of elaboration above a strong melody, a bass countermelody, and a repeated chord accompaniment.

Figure 25.8.   Elaboration as an Element of Musical Texture

OSTINATO

Another textural element that composers employ is the *ostinato*. The ostinato is a melodic pattern that is repeated again and again without change, usually in the bass. Traditional ostinato patterns are four or eight measures long, but shorter patterns are also quite common. A simple example from Persichetti's Serenade No. 7[3] is shown in Figure 25.9. The left hand plays a repeated four-note ostinato against the principal melody in the upper voice.

The ostinato bass was a favorite device in baroque music, especially in that of Purcell and Bach. The aria "When I Am Laid in Earth," from Purcell's *Dido and Aeneas* is a famous example, as is Bach's great Passacaglia in C minor for organ.

[3] Permission for reprint granted by Elkan-Vogel Co., Inc., Philadelphia, Pa. 19103, copyright owner.

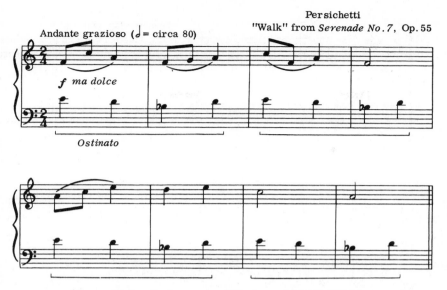

Figure 25.9. Ostinato as an Element of Musical Texture

EXTENDED PEDAL POINT

It will be helpful if an extended pedal point is treated as a separate textural element like the ostinato. Although a brief pedal point may easily be analyzed as a non-harmonic tone, some composers use such lengthy pedal points that the term *non-harmonic tone* ceases to be meaningful. Brahms, for instance, utilizes a pedal point in the *German Requiem* that continues all through a long fugue. Such a pedal point is more reasonably considered as a separate element of musical texture that is unrelated to the changes of harmony that occur in the music. Pedal points are present in several examples in this chapter. In Figure 25.2a, the A in the left hand is a pedal point. In Figure 25.4, the pedal point is a C, held steadily in one voice, but repeated rhythmically in another. Pedal points may also be seen in Figures 25.13, 25.14, and 25.15.

CHORDAL MOTIVE

Occasionally composers write sections of music whose principal interest is not melodic but harmonic. Instead of a melodic motive, such music has a *chordal motive*, which must be counted as a separate element of the musical texture. A well-known example is the beginning of the second movement of Dvořák's "New World" Symphony, shown in Figure 25.10. The melodic line in these few measures is insignificant; the real interest is in the harmonic progression. A similar example is the introduction to Grieg's song *From Monte Pincio*, shown in Figure 25.11.

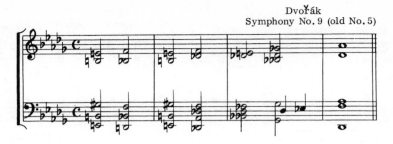

Figure 25.10. Chordal Motive in an Orchestral Work

Figure 25.11. Chordal Motive in a Song Accompaniment

REINFORCEMENT

One other textural element should be mentioned, although its use is normally limited to orchestral writing; this is *reinforcement*. Reinforcement is the momentary addition of instruments to the total textural pattern for the purpose of creating accent or of obtaining a better spacing of chord tones. Its function is solely that of emphasizing or clarifying the textural elements already present.

Reinforcement also occurs in keyboard music, although it is more difficult to recognize there than in orchestral music. In keyboard music, reinforcement is accomplished by increasing the density of tones in accented chords. For example, in a piece where most chords have only three or four tones, a chord with more doubling, having six to eight tones, will suddenly seem stronger; it has been reinforced by the addition of the doubled tones. Individual tones in a melodic line may similarly be reinforced in keyboard music by doubling only the notes to be accented. In these cases, reinforcement is a means of concentrating the attention of the listener on certain portions of the music.

Two kinds of reinforcement may be seen in the "Trepak" from the *Nutcracker Suite*. In the textural analysis shown in Figure 25.12, the first kind of reinforcement is played by instruments that join only for the accented note and the three pickup notes. The second element of reinforcement consists of chords played by the brass instruments only at the points of accent.

Figure 25.12. Reinforcement as a Textural Element

TEXTURAL ANALYSIS

A textural analysis of a piece of music is often helpful in understanding the structure of the work. It can therefore be instructive in composing music. A textural analysis requires that the separate textural elements of a piece be identified. The simplest procedure is to write each element on its own staff or staves. Figure 25.13 is the textural analysis of a piece with very few textural elements. This is the principal theme of the slow movement of Dvořák's "New World" Symphony. There are only three textural elements—a melody, an accompaniment that is largely harmonic, and a pedal point. A close examination of the orchestral score of this excerpt will show very smooth voice leading in the harmonic accompaniment. At no time, however, does any one voice in the accompaniment become significant enough to be treated as a countermelody.

Figure 25.13. Example of Textural Analysis

A more complex example of textural analysis is given in Figure 25.14, an analysis of a brief portion of Rimsky-Korsakov's *Scheherazade*.[4] In addition to the melody, there are three separate accompaniments, a pedal point, and reinforcement.

Figure 25.15 shows a similar textural analysis for three measures from the Sibelius Symphony No. 2.[5] The textural elements are, from top downward, melody, melodic doubling at the octave, first accompaniment (harmonic), second accompaniment (rhythmic), reinforcement, and pedal point.

---

[4] Reprinted from the Eulenberg Pocket Score of the complete *Scheherazade* with permission of C. F. Peters Corporation, New York, N.Y. 10016.

[5] Copyright 1903, 1931 by Breitkopf and Härtel, Wiesbaden. All rights reserved. Used by permission.

Rimsky-Korsakov
Scheherazade

Figure 25.14.   Analysis of a Complex Musical Texture

Figure 25.15. Analysis of a Complex Musical Texture

ESSENTIAL VOCABULARY

1. melodic doubling
2. melodic *broderie*
3. melodic outlining
4. ostinato
5. pedal point

6. elaboration
7. chordal motive
8. reinforcement
9. textural analysis

ASSIGNMENTS

1. Make a textural analysis like those shown in this chapter for each of the following sections of music:

  a) Schumann: *The Merry Farmer*, Op. 68, No. 10.
  b) Mozart: Piano Sonata No. 5, G major (K. 189h)
        Second Movement, measures 1–14.
  c) Mozart: Piano Sonata No. 9, D major (K. 205b)
        First Movement, measures 1–21.
  d) Beethoven: Piano Sonata, D major, Op. 28
        Second Movement, measures 1–22.

2. Arrange the melodies in Figure 19.21 on page 187 for piano so that they contain at least melody, countermelody, and an accompaniment. Add any other textural devices you wish, but make certain that the result is playable.

3. Write a short piece for piano in double period form, using the elements of texture you have studied.

APPENDIX

Writing Music
Manuscript

WRITING MUSIC MANUSCRIPT is a fairly simple process with a little practice and a few inexpensive tools. It is essential to have the proper size manuscript paper—some music publishers have as many as twenty different sizes. Each size has its own particular purpose, so choose yours carefully with the help of your teacher. A straight-edge ruler is helpful for drawing lines and planning page layout; many students also find a small draftsman's triangle helpful and convenient.

Special manuscript pens are available, although they are rather expensive and require some skill for their proper use. An ordinary fountain pen with either a broad point or an italic point is quite satisfactory for student work. Music manuscript looks much better written with black ink, rather than blue-black; india ink should never be used in ordinary fountain pens because it causes corrosion. A draftsman's ruling pen is the most satisfactory instrument for making long lines, such as bar lines.

A pen or pencil should be held differently when writing music than when writing words. Hold the pen between the index and middle fingers, steadying it with the thumb. The fourth and fifth fingers should be kept out of the way, close to the palm of the hand, so that the pen can be almost parallel to the paper, with the point headed due left. This position seems awkward at first, but becomes easy with practice.

WRITING THE CLEFS

The symbol for treble clef is usually written in two strokes, both of which start at the top, as shown in Illustration 26.1. It is important that the large loop in the second stroke be centered on the second line of the staff.

| 1 | 2 | 1+2 |

Illustration 26.1

The symbol for bass clef starts on the fourth line and is drawn in a clockwise direction, as shown by the arrow in Illustration 26.2. The two dots are important additions because they clearly mark the line intended as F.

Illustration 26.2

The symbol for alto and tenor clefs is made in the four strokes shown in Illustration 26.3.

| 1 | 2 | 3 | 4 | all strokes |

Illustration 26.3

WRITING NOTES AND RESTS

Notes and rests must be carefully written; they are made freehand, using firm, definite strokes. Note stems should not slant at all, but should be exactly vertical. Note stems are always made with a downward stroke, regardless of their position; moreover, the stem should come to a definite stop rather than taper away to nothing. White note heads such as the whole and half note are made in two strokes: 1) ⌒ plus 2) ⌣ results in ◯. The note is then easier to place accurately on the staff than if it were made in a single motion. With a pencil, black note heads are made with a short, heavy diagonal line. When using ink, the note head is made in two curved strokes so close together that the space in the center will be filled with ink: 1) ⌒ plus 2) ⌣ plus 3) | results in ♩.

If a note is dotted, the dot is placed just to the right of the note. If the note is on a line, the dot is placed in the space just above the line.

A quarter note rest, which at first seems awkward to draw, is most easily made by mentally altering a backward letter Z. In our thinking we first have ⅀ , then ⌇ , then finally 𝄽 .

INSERTING LEDGER LINES

Ledger lines are short lines above or below the staff, long enough for only a single note. They are spaced the same distance apart as the ordinary lines of the staff. Only enough ledger lines are used to reach a note; they are never written above or below a note that is off the staff, as is shown in Figure 26.1.

Right

Wrong

Figure 26.1

PLACING STEMS

When notes are written on a staff, the stems should be placed very carefully. When only one melodic line occurs on a staff, stems extend upward from the notes that are below the third line of the staff. Notes placed on the third line or higher have their stems extending downward, as in Figure 26.2. The length of the stems should be approximately the same as the height of three spaces of the staff.

Figure 26.2

If two melodic lines are placed on the same staff, a different usage is followed. Stems for the notes in the upper melodic line extend upward, regardless of where they fall on the staff; those for the lower melody extend downward, even if the two melodies temporarily cross. See Figure 26.3.

Figure 26.3

Music for keyboard instruments utilizes stems to indicate the right or left hand, or to delineate melodic lines in a complex musical texture. Figure 26.4 illustrates the use of ascending stems to denote the right hand, although the notes to be played are in the lower clef. In Figure 26.5 separate melodic lines are shown by the use of note stems, a procedure that is especially useful when a single note pertains to both of two separate elements of the musical texture.

It is difficult to indicate more than two voices on a single staff by the use of stems, especially if the voices have such wide ranges that they cross each other. In cases of this sort, it is sometimes possible to pair two voices to a stem. If this does not eliminate the confusion, it may be necessary to add an extra staff, even in keyboard music. The best use of stems is that which makes the music as clear as possible to the performer.

Figure 26.4.   The Use of Stems to Indicate Right or Left Hand

Figure 26.5.   The Use of Stems to Show Different Melodic Lines

In hymnals or other song books in which words are placed between the staves, all stems are kept away from the text unless it is necessary to show some special melodic movement. This notation is satisfactory only for simple music, such as that in Figure 26.6.

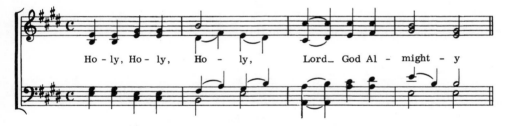

Figure 26.6.   Use of Stems in Hymnals

INSERTING ACCIDENTALS

When an accidental is used with a note, it is carefully placed on the same line or space of the staff as is the note itself. Accidentals are always placed to the left of the note head. When several accidentals occur before closely spaced notes, they should be staggered for the purpose of clarity, as shown in Figure 26.7.

Figure 26.7

In most music, an accidental affects its note for the remainder of the measure in which it occurs. Some pieces of twentieth century music state that accidentals apply only to the single notes on which they occur. When an accidental is cancelled, the change should be indicated the first time that note reoccurs in its original form, even though it is several measures later.

INDEX

A, standard frequency of, 15n
Absolute pitch, 79
Accent, 32
Accidentals:
    duration, 256
    effect on key, 116-17
    in key signatures, 73-75, 90-92
    in minor keys, 92-95
    placement of, 255-56
    symbols for, 14
Accompaniment, 150, 156-59, 228-36
    arpeggiated, 232-33
    broken chord, 231-32
    harmonic, 156-57
    harmonic and rhythmic, 158-59
    in hymns, 157
    repeated chord, 230-31
    rhythmic, 157-58
    sustained chord, 230
    "um-pah-pah," 234
Adagio, 43
Aeolian mode, 90
Alberti bass, 233
Allegro, 43
Altered tones:
    diatonic, 100
    effect on key, 117
    in minor, 92-94
Alto clef, 17
Alto voice, range, 191
Amen cadence, 120
Amplitude, 11
Anacrusis, 39
Analysis:
    functional, 84-85, 98-99, 106-7
    root/quality, 61, 108
    textural, 247-50
Andante, 43
Anglican chant, 164-65
Antecedent phrase, 137
Anticipation, 223-24
Appoggiatura, 126n, 222-23
Arpeggiated six-four chord, 217
Arts, study of, 7
Augmentation, 166
Augmented interval, 50
Augmented triad, 59-60
Authentic cadence, 117-18
Auxiliary tone, 127

Bach, J. S.:
    Cantata No. 78, *Jesu, der du meine Seele*,
        154
    chorales, 94-95, 107, 118, 120, 121, 144-
        46, 172, 177, 190, 204-5
    Fuga sopra il Magnificat, 153
    Fugue in G minor, 151
    Goldberg Variations, 141
    Invention in D minor, 155

Passacaglia in C minor, 244
    Well-Tempered Clavier, 36
Bar line, 27
Baritone clef, 17
Bartók, Béla:
    Mikrokosmos, 41-42
    *Music for String Instruments, Percussion,
        and Celesta*, 41, 240-41
Bass:
    Alberti, 233
    alternating, 218
    figured, 154, 200-205
    realizing a, 200, 205
    rocking, 218
    writing a, 182-84
Bass clef, 17
Bass part, 61
Bass voice, range, 191
Basso continuo, 154, 200
Basso ostinato, 244-45
Bass suspension, 128
Beam, 33
Beat:
    compound, 28
    conductor's, 34-35
    in dancing, 24
    nature of, 24
    simple, 28
    types, 28
Beat unit, 25
    for compound beats, 28
Beats, strong and weak, 32
Beethoven, Ludwig van:
    Diabelli Variations, 141
    Die Ehre Gottes aus der Natur, 230-31
    "Eroica" Variations, 153
    Mignon, 229
    Minuet in G, 217
    Sonata for Piano, Op. 2, No. 1, 139-40
    Sonata for Piano, Op. 13, 177-78
    Sonata for Piano, Op. 14, No. 1, 180
    Sonata for Piano, Op. 26, 119, 138-39
    Sonata for Piano, Op. 31, No. 1, 39
    Sonata for Piano, Op. 106, 239
    Symphony No. 3, 152
    Symphony No. 5, 141
    Symphony No. 7, 141
    Symphony No. 8, 163
*Believe Me if All Those Endearing Young
    Charms*, 172
Brahms, Johannes:
    Denn es gehet, 116
    German Requiem, 225, 245
    Symphony No. 1, 166
    Symphony No. 2, 176
    Symphony No. 4, 136, 155, 176
    Variations on a Theme by Haydn, 141
Breve, 25
Broderie, melodic, 242-43

Interval *(cont.)*
  inversion, 54
  major, 50
  melodic, 49
  minor, 50
  name, 49
  perfect, 50
  quality, 50, 51-53
  simple, 54
Interval alteration, 166
Intervals, addition of, 53
Inversion:
  first, 62
  of interval, 54
  of motive, 166
  second, 62
  of tetrads, 106
  third, 106
  of triads, 61
Inverted pedal point, 224
Irregular resolution, 86

Jaques-Dalcroze, Émile, 42

Key, 71
  changing (*See* Modulation)
  establishing a, 115-17
  major, 71-77
  minor, 90-96
Keyboard, diagram of, 15
Keynote, 70
Keys:
  closely related, 143
  parallel, 92
  relative, 92
Key signatures:
  circle of fifths, 74-75, 92
  major, 73
  minor, 90
  order of flats, 74
  order of sharps, 74

Languages, study of, 7
Large forms, 140-41
Leading tone, 73-76, 93-96
Leading tone chord, 218-19
Lead sheet, 200
Learning, as physical skill, 4
Ledger lines, 16
  how to write, 253-54
Legato, 26n
Light, speed of, 10
Listening, learning skill of, 5
  during practice, 5
Loudness, 11
  acoustic levels of, 12
  musical levels of, 13
  unit of, 12

M. M., 43
McHose, Allen I., 71n
Major interval, 50
Major key signatures, 73
Major-minor seventh chord, 104
Major mode, 71

Major scale, 71-73, 75-77
Major triad, 59
Mälzel, Johann, 43
Manuscript, writing music, 253-56
Masculine cadence, 117
Measure, 27
  asymmetrical division of, 41
Measure line, 27
Measures, counting, 39
Mediant tone, 73, 75-76, 94-95
Mediant triad, 85, 105, 213-17
Melodic *broderie,* 242-43
Melodic doubling, 238-41
Melodic minor scale, 93n
Melodic outlining, 243
Melody:
  analysis, 161-67
  chant, 164-65
  chord choice for, 169-72
  coherence in, 161
  doubling a, 178
  emphasis in, 161
  harmonizing, 169-72
  harmony implied by, 162-63
  motivic, 164, 167-68
  non-harmonic tones in, 162-63
  song, 164-66
  textural element, 150-59
  types, 164-67
  unity in, 161
  writing bass for, 175-84
Mendelssohn, Felix, Symphony No. 4, 164
Meter, 27-31, 40-42
  asymmetrical, 41
  changing, 40
  definition, 27
  in different time signatures, 30
  duple, 27
  in modern music, 40-42
  quadruple, 27
  single, 27
  triple, 27
Metronome, 7, 43
Metronome markings, 43
Mezzo forte, 13
Mezzo piano, 13
Mezzo-soprano clef, 18
Minim, 25
Minor interval, 50
Minor key signatures, 90
Minor mode, 71, 90
Minor scale, 90-96
  composite, 93
  harmonic, 93n
  melodic, 93n
  natural, 91
  ten-tone, 93
  tones of, 93-94
Minor triad, 59-60
Mode:
  Aeolian, 90
  definition, 71, 115
  Dorian, 71
  major, 71
  minor, 71, 90
  Phrygian, 71
Modulation, 143-46
  duration, 143-45